Project Management

The Managerial Aspects

Project Management

The Managerial Aspects

G.P. Sudhakar
Associate Professor,
The ICFAI University, Hyderabad, India

New Century Publications
New Delhi, India

NEW CENTURY PUBLICATIONS
4800 / 24, Bharat Ram Road,
Ansari Road, Daryaganj,
New Delhi - 110 002 (India)

Tel.: 011 - 4358 7398, 4101 7798, 2324 7798

Email: info@newcenturypublications.com

www.newcenturypublications.com

Editorial office:
4832/24, Ansari Road, Daryaganj,
New Delhi – 110 002

Tel.: 011-4356 0919

First Published: **2020**

ISBN: **978-81-7708-515-0**

Published by New Century Publications and printed at Milan Enterprises, New Delhi.

Designs: Patch Creative Unit, New Delhi.

PRINTED IN INDIA

About the Book

Poor project management and execution leads to considerable wastage of resources on the part of business enterprises. This indicates the need for a systematic study of project management techniques. Knowledge, skills, experience, leadership and competencies of a project manager impact the success of a project. Learning project management from macro management point of view can increase the success rate of a project.

This book provides insights into various concepts, definitions, research findings, industry best practices, tools and techniques for project management and scope for further research. In short, it is intended to provide systematically arranged authentic information on managerial dimensions of project management.

The book is organized into 3 parts:

Part I (chapters 1 to 6) is titled Strategy and Project Management. Apart from introduction to managerial aspects of project management, it covers topics such as basics of project strategy, characteristics of content development projects, nature of work of a global manager, role of conflicts in top management teams, and a case study of Tata Group.

Part II (chapters 7 to 13) is titled Project Management Research. It deals with such topics as project success requirements, success factors for software projects, conflict management techniques, lessons from *Bhagavad Gita* in project management, success factors for offshore software development projects, scientific versus social science research methodology, and research in management.

Part III (chapters 14 to 20) is titled People Aspects in Project Management. It is devoted to explanation and examination of different dimensions of teams, performance of software development teams, recruitment strategies of Indian IT firms, software programmers, software organizations, and project stakeholders and technology.

About the Author

Dr. G.P. Sudhakar is Associate Professor, The ICFAI University, Hyderabad, India. He has 24 years of professional experience, with 12 years in IT industry and 12 years in academics/research. Earlier, he worked as senior faculty member and head of IT Division at Engineering Staff College of India, Hyderabad. He has also worked in US, UK, Ireland, and Finland. He also holds M.Tech. and Executive MBA. He is also a Project Management Professional certified by Project Management Institute (PMI), USA since 2006.

Dr. Sudhakar has authored 15 books and published over 100 research papers/case studies in academic journals of repute including *International Journal of Project Management Research* (Netherlands), *Brazilian Journal of Production and Operations Management* (Brazil), *Serbian Journal of Management* (Serbia), *Team Performance Management* (Emerald, UK), and *Binus Business Review* (Indonesia).

His areas of research interest include project management, critical success factors, conflict management, software engineering, and innovative research methodologies.

This book is dedicated to all organizations, institutions,
universities, colleges, schools, journals, industry
bodies, professional associations in India
and abroad from whom I learned
management theory and practice

Contents

Part II: Project Management Research

Part III: People Aspects in Project Management

Preface

A project is a temporary endeavour undertaken to create a unique product, service or result. A project has certain characteristics. Every project has a specified goal or objective. Stakeholders of a project are impacted by its outcome—positive or negative. Every project has limited time and budget allocation. Every project comes with opportunities and risks. It is the project manager who has to exploit the opportunity and mitigate the project risks. Project success leads to commercial success for an organization. Project is executed by a designated team. Different team members play different roles, contributing to the success of the project. Project manager has to apply his skills, knowledge and experience in leading the project to success.

Poor project management and execution leads to considerable wastage of resources on the part of business enterprises. This indicates the need for a systematic study of project management techniques. Knowledge, skills, experience, leadership and competencies of a project manager impact the success of a project. Learning project management from macro management point of view can increase the success rate of a project.

Project strategy is the set of actions to keep project in-line with business strategy of an organization in order to make project outcome contribute to its progress. Project governance is the umbrella framework in-between organizational strategy and organizational performance, comprising project portfolios, setting project directions, governing and evaluating the progress.

Project management office (PMO) is the management structure which provides guidance, tools, techniques, project management standards, and needed support to the projects and also monitors the project progress by collecting regular project metrics.

Project management research areas include: project management frameworks, project management conceptual models, project complexity, project size, project leader behaviour, project team behaviour, project benefits, project scheduling, and project risk management.

With the growing global spending on projects, and increasing gap between demand and supply of project managers, the need for building project management skills and competencies cannot be under estimated. The project management standards, practices and applications are becoming global in nature.

The present work is intended to provide systematically arranged authentic information on managerial dimensions of project management.

Acknowledgements

I would like to thank my university The ICFAI University, Hyderabad; its different schools including ICFAI Research Centre, ICFAI School of HRD, ICFAI School of IT, and ICFAI Law School.

I would also like to thank my previous associations including Engineering Staff College of India (ESCI), Hyderabad and Aurora Group of Institutions, Hyderabad.

In industry, I would like to thank organizations where I was associated on full-time/in consultant capacity including Canarys Automations, Siemens Information Systems Ltd. (SISL), IBM India Software Lab, Raffles Software, Interwoven, Bangalore and Wipro Technologies.

Above all, I place on record my deep affection and regard for my family who supported me in different walks of my life, in particular, Manju, Manasa, Shruti, my mother Bhramaramba Devi, and late father and teacher Sarma.

Hyderabad **Goparaju Purna Sudhakar**
July 2020

Part I
Strategy and Project Management

1

Introduction to Managerial Aspects of Project Management

1.1 What is a Project?

According to PMI-PMBOK (Project Management Body of Knowledge), "A project is a temporary endeavour undertaken to create a unique product, service or result".

A project has certain characteristics. Every project has a specified goal or objective. A project has a beginning and an end date. A project outcome has either positive or negative impacts for its stakeholders. Project stakeholders influence the project either positively or negatively. Every project has limited time and budget allocation. There is no project with unlimited time and finances. Every project comes with opportunity and also with risks. It is the project manager who has to exploit the opportunity and mitigate the project risks. Project success may lead to commercial success/benefits or financial benefits for an organization undertaking it.

Project is executed by a designated team. Different team members in the project team play different roles contributing to the project success/project performance. Project manager has to apply his skills, knowledge and experience in leading the project for success. Every project has got certain complexities. Project outcome is a product, service or result.

Following are the examples of recently undertaken, ongoing or completed projects:

1. Gaganyan of Indian Space Research Organization (ISRO).
2. Statue of Unity.
3. Metro Rail Project, Hyderabad.
4. Konkan Railways Project.
5. International Airport Project, Bangalore.
6. Delhi Metro Rail Project.

7. Jamnagar Refinery, Reliance Industries.
8. Mumbai-Worli Sea Link Bridge.
9. Aadhar Project of Unique Identification Authority of India (UIDAI).
10. National Ganga River Basin Project.

1.2 What is Project Management?

Project management is application of knowledge, skills and experience in leading and executing a project. Project management involves project initiation, project planning, project execution, project monitoring and controlling, and project closing.

Project management is the way of implementing or realising organizational strategy. Project management is about planning, organizing, directing, leading, staffing, motivating, coordinating, and controlling the project. Project management is nothing but the application of basic management functions to the project.

In some of the organizations, project management is done by a project manager. In some others, it is the project management team which manages the project. It all depends on the size of project. In the case of a small project, a single project manager can handle it. For large/huge projects, a project management team is required to take care of the project.

Project management brings in aspects such as general management, operations and psychology, all under the same umbrella. In Figure 1.1, the darkness in each circle indicates the level of impact of that subject/area on project management. Psychology has little contribution, operations have moderate contribution, and general management has major contribution in the success of the project. In other words, it indicates the conceptual movement, number of concepts and applications from these respective areas into project management discipline.

Figure 1.1: Project Management as a Discipline

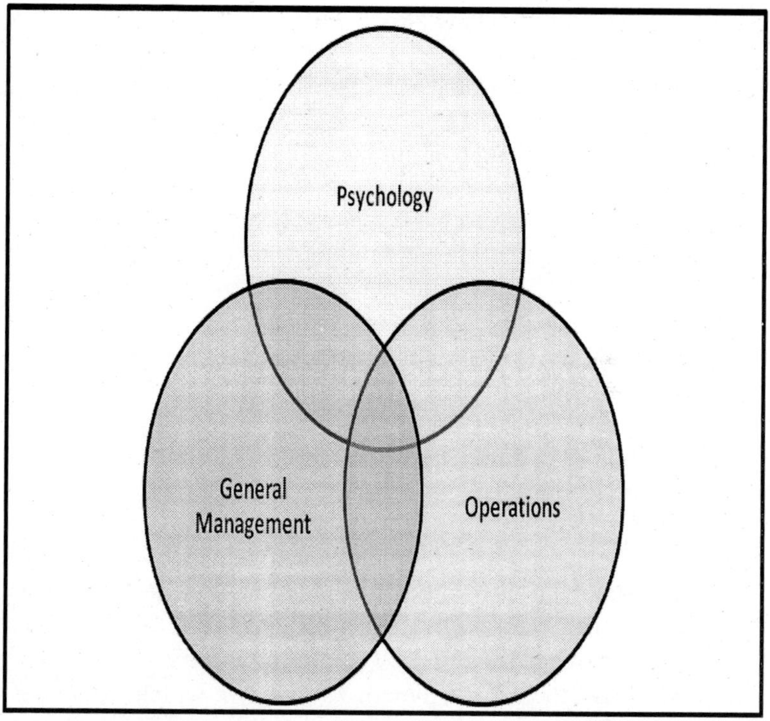

1.3 Project Management in India

With the growth of government projects since 2015, project management is gaining traction in India. It is expected to rise rapidly. India is going to create 7,00,000 project manager jobs between 2017 and 2027.

In India, project management best practices are used in automobiles and IT industries. Project management is more matured in these industries than other sectors.

The factors impacting Indian projects include the following:

1. Funding challenges.
2. Land acquisition issues.

3. Law and order problems.
4. Environmental clearances.
5. Delays in equipment supply.
6. Bad weather.
7. Technology selection.
8. Project contract related issues and litigations.

The major challenges in Indian projects include:

1. Inaccurate assessment of risks.
2. Lack of capability to manage complexity.
3. Inability in estimations and monitoring.
4. Difficulty involving multiple stakeholders.
5. Sync between project plan and execution.

To handle these challenges, project governance and project management play a major role.

1.4 Project Governance and Strategy

Project governance is about setting direction, taking decision on project implementation, and then overseeing the progress of the project. Thus, project governance comes with different roles in the framework involving project sponsor, project steering committee, project manager and project management office (PMO).

PMO is the management structure which provides guidance, tools, techniques, project management standards, and needed support to the projects and also monitors the project progress by collecting regular project metrics. PMO plays different roles in different organizations such as supportive PMO, directing PMO and controlling PMO. Decision-making in project governance includes listening, questioning, collecting evidence, authority and the decision-making process itself. The purpose of project governance is to control the projects in order to achieve business objectives. Project governance provides a link between organizational business strategy and project outcomes. Corporate governance includes organizational strategy which comprises of operational strategy in which project governance is a part.

Project strategy is the set of actions to keep project in-line with organizational business strategy in order to make project performance and outcome contribute to the organizational performance. Project strategy links organizational business strategies and performance. Project governance is the umbrella framework between organizational strategy and organizational performance comprising of project portfolios, setting project directions, governing and checking progress.

1.5. Project Management Research Areas

Project management research areas include the following:

1. Project management frameworks.
2. Project management conceptual models.
3. Project size and complexity.
4. Behaviour of project leader.
5. Behaviour of project team.
6. Project benefits, performance and success.
7. Project scheduling.
8. Project risk management.
9. Project vendor management.
10. Customer relationship.
11. Project procurements.
12. Project budgets and finances.

Research has proved that the more the project management maturity in an organization, the more is the project success rate and return on investment. Management consulting organizations across the world, such as KPMG, Accenture, PwC, and McKinsey, conduct global project management surveys and publish research reports in addition to the regular academic community doing project management research. Professional bodies/organizations such as PMI (Project Management Institute, USA), IPMA (International Project Management Association), and APM (Association of Project Management, UK) also conduct project management global surveys. For example, PMI Global Project Management Professionals Salary Survey is one of the popular researches across the world in the industry.

1.6 Project Management Frameworks and Models

Many researchers have tried to give conceptual frameworks for different branches of project management separately. For example, conceptual framework for the impact of human resources on project management, project risk management framework, and project management under uncertainty. However, conceptual frameworks and models for complete project management as a single whole are rarely discussed.

A framework gives a macro view of the project whereas a model gives a micro view involving the factors/components of project management.

It is important for project management framework to mention the following:

1. External environmental factors such as contractual environment.
2. Strategy factors such as operational strategy and marketing strategy.
3. Organizational factors such as reputation and organizational climate.
4. Internal team factors.
5. Industry and domain factors.

1.7. Human Aspects of Project Management

Every project is executed by a team of individuals. Some may do the actual work and some may monitor and delegate the tasks. However, at the end of the day, the project is carried out and completed by human beings. It may use some raw material, machinery and tools for the project-product development purpose. However, human beings play a major role in project planning and execution. These human beings include the project team, project manager, customer, vendor or supplier, and regulatory and financial institutions.

Every human being involved in the project has his own personal interests and priorities. Such things impact a project performance and success.

1.8 Project Teams

Project teams can be categorised as *project management team* and *project execution team.* This is just a logical categorization. This is because, in case of large projects, there are *project management teams* comprising of 2 or more project managers taking care of the responsibility of project planning, budgeting, scheduling and other monitoring and controlling activities.

Project execution team is the one which does the actual work. They work towards the project product/service/result development. Their tasks may be related to technical aspects of the project product being developed. Mostly, in literature, project team means the execution team which does the actual work.

Project team comes with certain skills, competencies, and knowledge. Project team exhibits certain attitudes and behaviour in dealing with customer and project manager. Project team's attitude and behaviour varies as the project progresses through different phases.

Trust plays a major role between project manager and project team in achieving the project targets. If trust is there, cohesion and collaboration will be there, if cohesion and collaboration towards task is present, it leads to project performance. When team members are chosen, it is the best practice to find somebody from project product-domain experts, some functional expert, and somebody who does the support activities.

Based on the project product/service being developed, team members from different functional departments are to be chosen for the project. In some organizations, based on product type, cross-disciplinary teams are also formed. Some of the team characteristics include team diversity, team composition, team roles, team size, team tenure, team task, team competency, team climate and team conflicts. The possible processes in a team environment include: team cohesion, team coordination, team collaboration, team communication, and team cooperation etc.

1.9 Project Control

Project control involves collecting project metrics, comparing the project performance with the expected results, and taking corrective action in case of any deviation. Project needs to be controlled at every phase exit. Mainly cost, time, quality and scope of a project need to be controlled. Key performance indicators (KPIs) can also be considered for measuring and controlling project performance. Some of the best practices with respect to project control include the following:

1. **Scope Control and Verification:** If project cost or time is adjusted, it is the best practice to revisit scope. This is because if time and cost change, scope of the project also needs to be changed.
2. **Cost Control:** Compare the project cost performance with the cost baseline created during project planning stage. Variance analysis can be applied to find out the cost variances. Here, actual cost, planned cost, budgeted cost, forecasted cost and approved cost are used for cost control in project.
3. **Schedule Control:** Schedule control can be done using network analysis, critical path method (CPM), resource levelling, leads and lags, schedule compression techniques etc.
4. **Quality Control:** It is the best practice to continuously improve the project product quality through incremental quality improvements. It is also better to measure the maturity level of quality in a project. It is important to have thrust on quality from top in an organization.
5. **Risk Control:** It is the best practice to keep monitoring not only the internal project environment but also the external project environment. It is the best practice to prioritize risks on basis of their impact and probability of occurrence in a project.
6. **Monitoring and Controlling Contracts:** It is the best practice to continuously review the procurements made

through contracts. Contract administration, checking contract performance, and assessment/measurement are required throughout the project. Whether all the deliverables are received and payments are made as per the control need to be verified.

7. **Stakeholder Engagement Control:** It is the best practice to analyse the interest and influence of each stakeholder. The project manager has to take corrective actions based on stakeholder influence level and interest level. Also the project manager should check the team management aspects such as team development and team control.

2

Basics of Project Strategy

Project management is meeting customer requirements with skills, knowledge and experience within the budget in provided time with good quality. Program management is managing related projects at the same time. This will be done by the program managers in an organization.

2.1 Individual Project Status Check

A project manager is responsible for the delivery of individual projects. He plans, executes, monitors and controls an individual project. He is responsible for the success of the project. The project status review (PSR) meetings are useful for checking the project progress. The project manager is responsible for project tracking as well. Individual project managers report their progress to the program manager. The project manager can use earned value management (EVM) techniques to check the deviations in time and cost. He can also use network diagrams for scheduling purposes.

The program progress is checked by the program manager based on individual project progress. The general information meetings (GIMs) are useful for communicating the program progress to the stakeholders. This is done by many well-known product development companies in mobile phone industry. The senior management review (SMR) meetings are useful to gather inputs from each project and consolidate them and prepare the progress of the program. For example, one project may depend on deliverables of another project. The output of a project may be an input for another project. These dependencies need to be checked and tracked by the program managers.

Definitely, a program manager has to have information about

all the projects in his program. In some organizations, requirements management, and feature selection for the product are also part of program management. An example for program may be development of a mobile phone. The hardware development becomes one project and the software development for the mobile phone becomes another project. However, these two projects are related. Hence, it is a program.

2.2 Risk Management

There can be risks common to all the projects in a program. These kinds of risks can be identified by the program manager and accordingly assign individual risks. It is easy to track if we identify the risks at the program level as well. Risk identification is a continuous process. A program manager is responsible for any cost and schedule over-runs of the program. That is why he has to track the respective projects closely and ensure the timely completion of the projects of the program. The quality of the program depends on quality of all the deliverables of the respective projects. Hence, project managers should ensure quality deliverables within the cost and within the time limits. For a majority of program managers, schedule overrun is a major area of concern.

2.3 Needed Skills for Program Management

Definitely, a program manager needs to have communication, decision-making and negotiation skills in addition to technical skills like features management for the product. In some IT MNCs, program management keeps product development, maintenance, and testing teams in their control in addition to the project management teams. In software services organizations, related customer projects are kept under one program. There are program managers in IT services firms such as Wipro and there are program managers in product development companies such as IBM.

Recently, Project Management Institute (PMI), USA has come up with a certification called PgMP (Program Management

Professional) for program managers who are working in different industries.

The projects handled by the program managers are related. Hence, the dependency between projects is one area of concern for program managers. The shuffling of human resources between the projects, budgetary constraints, and timelines are areas of concern for any program manager. Resource sharing between the project managers is also another area of concern for a program manager.

2.4 Prioritize the Projects

Once project data collection is over, it is time to prioritize the projects based on certain factors. Here, there are tools available to prioritize the projects of an organization. One such tool is weight impact matrix. The factors which affect each project include productivity, customer satisfaction, employee satisfaction, risk, profitability, and return on investment etc. In prioritizing the projects, the first step is to assign a certain weight (between 0 and 1) to each of these factors, which affect the projects. For each project against each factor, assign a score ranging from 1 to 10: 1 being the minimum and 10 being the maximum. For example, the weight of customer satisfaction is 0.8, and the impact of this factor for project X could be 8 on a scale of 1 to 10. Then, multiply the weight with impact and sum all these values for all the factors, which results in a numeric figure. The project with maximum value of this figure is the top priority project for an organization. An example for weight impact matrix is given in Table 2.1.

As shown in Table 2.1, project 2 has got the maximum score in weight impact matrix. Hence, we need to give top priority to project 2. Like this, we can prioritize our portfolio of projects so that the senior management can concentrate on top priority projects, and provide the funding and resources to the top priority projects in the organization.

Once we identify the top priority projects in the organization, it is time to invest resources and money in them.

We need to assess the foreseen risks for the projects as well while collecting the projects details and prioritize them.

Table 2.1: Weight Impact Matrix

Impact Area	Weight	Project 1	Project 2	Project 3
Customer Satisfaction	0.9	8	9	7
Employee Satisfaction	0.9	6	8	8
Productivity	0.8	7	7	5
ROI	0.7	7	8	6
Profitability	0.8	8	7	7
....				
....				
....				
Total Weight Impact Score		29.5	32.1	27.3

2.5 Maintaining a Resource Pool

The first thing, in planning for an enterprise-wide project management solution is to build a resource pool in the organization. We need to gather all the human resources, who are eligible for allocation to projects, and they need to be gathered and stored in a database. The resource pool should consist of information like names of the employees, their department or group, email IDs, their manager, and their role in the organization, etc.

This resource pool is useful to create individual project plans and task assignments. The project and portfolio managers should have access to these resource pools in the organization in addition to resource managers. The resource pools are useful to get the weekly timesheets and to find out the task engagements of the resources.

2.6 Evaluation of the EPM Tools

Next step is to evaluate the enterprise project management (EPM) tools, which are available in the market. Some of them are

Microsoft Enterprise Project Management Solution, Computer Associate's Clarity, and Primavera etc. Microsoft's Enterprise Project Management Solution comes with Microsoft Project Server 2007 and Microsoft Portfolio Server 2007 with their respective clients including Web Access and Microsoft Project Professional 2007. The evaluation can be done based on parameters such as reliability, effectiveness, and easy to operate.

After evaluation of the EPM tools, one can suggest a suitable EPM tool for an organization.

Once it is decided to use a suitable EPM tool for the organization, the first step is to install and configure the enterprise project management tool. Once installation is done, we need to create a resource pool of the organization in the tool. This will be stored in the tool's underlying database. Then, it is our job to have a pilot run. Take any project in the organization and upload the project details into the system. It is the responsibility of the respective project manager or the project leader. Let this team use the system on a pilot basis. Based on the needs of the team, we may have to modify the configuration settings in the EPM tool. Resultantly, it is live for the entire organization. Using the current day EPM tools, one can even maintain the timesheets, risks, issues and project documents in the EPM system. The portfolio managers can get the dashboard of the projects.

Once configuration, upload of resource details, and project details are completed, the enterprise project management tool is operational and the entire organization can make use of this project management tool.

Following this, it depends on the project manager's knowledge, skills and experience in estimating the tasks and project. The project managers will be able to track the progress using these EPM tools. Usually, they provide percentage (%) completion of the tasks and projects. The portfolio manager gets a dashboard of all the projects and their status. He can even see the cost estimated, the actual cost spent on the projects, the schedule and the cost overrun of the projects.

2.7 Identification of Stakeholders

While developing a project charter, the project manager should identify the stakeholders of the project. This is a very important step in project management. Actually, stakeholder identification is a continuous process. At any stage of the project, stakeholders can be identified. Hence, it is the best practice to discover the stakeholders list and document it at the initial stages of the project. During the course of the project, the stakeholders list can be updated. Because, different stakeholders will have different wants and needs, the project manager should be aware of the needs and wants of the stakeholders. This makes the job of a project manager easy and reduces future conflicts in the project.

2.8 Project Planning

Once project charter is approved by the customer or senior management, the project manager can go ahead with project planning. For doing project planning, the project manager can use work breakdown structures (WBS) as a tool. Once the work packages, control accounts and planning packages are identified from the work breakdown structure, the project manager can go ahead with project scheduling. Before this, the project manager has to identify the resources needed for the project, both human and machinery such as hardware and software.

During the project planning stage, for scheduling purposes, tools such as Microsoft Project or Primavera can be used. During planning stage, one can identify critical paths in the network diagram during schedule development. We can also identify the risks involved using critical path in the network diagram. During schedule development, the project manager can use different schedule compression techniques such as crashing and fast tracking.

2.9 Communicating the Project Plan

Once the project plan is made, it is the job of the project

manager to communicate this to all the stakeholders. In the early stages of project, the project manager has already identified the stakeholders. This project plan needs to be communicated to all the identified stakeholders. At the same time, not all stakeholders are interested in all the information of the project. The project manager has to maintain the details of who needs what information in the communications management plan. Based on the communications management plan, the project manager needs to distribute the information to the stakeholders. Like this, the project manager communicates the project plan to the stakeholders. This avoids confusion in the future and everybody would be aware of the goals and objectives of the project.

Usually at the beginning of the project, the objectives are set to the project from organization point of view. At the same time, the objectives are to be set at the individual level as well. Some of the companies such as Tata Consultancy Services do this by using Balanced Score Cards (BSC) for setting objectives for the team members by drilling down the objectives at organizational, departmental, and project level. This objective setting process is very important because the team members are made aware about what is expected out of them. Usually, the objectives will be set in technical areas as well as managerial areas (if any) for the team members.

2.10 Project Execution

The project manager should get the approval for the project plan. It may be in the form of a sign off from the customer, if the customer decides the project deadlines. Otherwise, if it is an internal project, the project manager should get approval from the senior management for the project plan. Once project plan is approved, the project manager should go for project execution. By this time, some of the resources might have been allocated already for the project. Using the allocated resources, the project manager should execute the project.

Usually, a majority of times, project managers spend time

in execution of the projects with the help of a team, if it is a long duration project.

In the execution stage of the project, the progress needs to be tracked. The project manager using different tools and techniques such as earned values, decision trees and statistical control techniques tracks the project progress. The project manager has to update the senior management whether the project is on time, under budget or if there are any deviations from the planned details. Cost variance and schedule variance also needs to be updated in the project plan.

While tracking the progress, the project manager conducts project status review (PSR) meetings periodically with weekly frequency, usually.

2.11 Evaluating Team Member Performance

At the end of the project or at the end of appraisal period, the performance of the team members should be evaluated as is done for project appraisals. The objective of performance appraisals is to identify the training needs of the candidates and to take necessary actions. The effect of performance appraisal will be there on human resource activities such as promotions, transfers, demotions and exits. In all these cases, the human resource department needs to take necessary actions. In IT organizations, usually, the rating scale method is used for programmer's performance appraisals. If the number of employees is very less, then we can even go for ranking method of performance appraisals.

The project manager may not wait for the performance appraisal time to come to give feedback to the team members. A good project manager gives feedback to the team members at regular intervals and observes the progress of the team members. He helps in the advancement of his team members. If the needed progress is not observed in a team member, then the project manager needs to take necessary action against the team member. This comes under the controlling function of the project manager.

The project manager has to update the senior management and other stakeholders with the status of the project. The frequency of this status reporting to the senior management varies from organization to organization. Some organizations conduct this senior management review (SMR) meetings once in a month. Also, the project needs to under go periodic quality audits from the quality department. The project manager is responsible for closing the non-conformances (NCs) given by the QA team. Usually, the organization-wide QA team tracks these open NCs of all the projects in an organization. This happens because the QA team is responsible for internal and external audits of the organization.

While executing the project, the project manager may face some risks or unexpected circumstances. Hence, it is better to do risk planning as part of project planning. Identification of risks, qualitative and quantitative risk analysis and risk response planning and risk monitoring and control are the steps involved in risk management. Hence, with proper risk management, the project manager will be in a position to execute the project smoothly.

Also if something goes wrong, the project manager should be able to check the health of the project and rescue the project.

2.12 Training and Development

Based on the performance appraisals, the training and development needs will be identified and planned. The training needs vary from individual to individual. Based on these training needs, the project manager has to update the training plan. The human resources department will issue the training calendar after they receive inputs from all the project managers. It is better for the individuals to attend the scheduled training programs for his/her development purposes.

Usually, there are different types of trainings, which can be provided to the team members. Some of them are induction, on the job training, coaching, and hands on training. The internal or external faculty can provide the training programs.

The training needs for engineers and managers vary. Based on the experience level of the team member and the project needs, the project manager should nominate a candidate for the training programs.

2.13 Releasing the Deliverables

Once the deliverables are ready, that is, after all internal and external (if any) reviews, the project manager has to hand over the same to the customer. The customer may in turn do acceptance testing of the deliverables. This is the scenario in any turnkey solution or a typical project environment. If the project deliverable is a product, then the project manager has to release the deliverables and related documentation to the customer support team. Because, once the product is released from the engineering team, it is the responsibility of the support team to provide support for the product. While handing over the product to the support team, the engineering team should execute knowledge transfer to the support team.

Once the product is handed over to the customer support or technical support team, the project manager has the responsibility of closing the project officially.

He has to do the post-mortem of the project. The project manager has to document the lessons learnt during the course of the project. He has to subsequently release all the human resources attached with the project. Finally, the project manager has to officially communicate about the closure of the project to all the stakeholders concerned.

3

Program Management of Content Development Projects

Program management in content development industry is very challenging because of the low budget projects. The success of the content development program depends on *successful project management*. The program manager has to have exceptional people with skills in this industry.

3.1. Introduction

Content development is one of the emerging areas in global economy. With the advancements in technology, mergers and acquisitions, innovations, changing learning styles and needs, and growing education sector, these areas have been the sources of new projects in content development. With changing publishing styles and launch of devices such as tablet, kindle, e-book, smart reader, smart phone and other smart devices, the content is getting customized across the globe. There are many success factors for content development projects:

1. Absence of plagiarism.
2. Timely delivery.
3. Relevance to current needs.
4. Richness of content.
5. Variety in contents such as figures, diagrams, images, tables, graphs etc.
6. Uniqueness in content.

All these things should be possible within a given budget. However, there are many challenges in executing content development programs both in industry and academia.

3.2 Uniqueness of Content Development Projects

Content development projects are unique in certain ways.

No two content development products are same. However, up to some extent, overlap is possible in content development products. In other words, some sections or figures or diagrams can be the same in two or many content products. This has to be dealt with *reuse* approach. Content development projects also have time limits. The very special character across the world in content development projects is that these projects are highly low budgeted projects. It is a challenge for both the program manager and project manager to get the things done on time, in budget with acceptable quality without plagiarism.

Also, the content development skills remain with majority of baby boomers in academia in many countries. However, there do exist a few X and Y generation individuals in content development industry. You may rarely find a Z generation or a millennial in this industry (this group is more active in social media rather than formal content development). This trend brings in many human resources challenges to the program and project managers.

The content development project starts with a set of requirements, goes on into literature review, industry product reviews, domain specific reviews, review of author experiences, perspectives from content development team and reviewers, operations and production team and finally the learners or readers.

3.3 Content Development Program Planning

Usually, content development goes as program in any academic institution or industry. There are multiple related projects getting executed simultaneously. There are dependencies in schedules and costs between projects within the program. For example, a program of content development in an academic institution starts with curriculum development for a specific program such as MBA, post-graduate diploma, diploma or a certificate program. This curriculum development itself is a group task if you are planning to develop content in advanced or niche areas. The team consists of very specialized researchers, academicians and industry experts. The academic program curriculum consists of different courses or subjects from which the actual content has to be developed. The curriculum also undergoes both internal and external reviews.

The program manager of content development team has to take the curriculum as an input for the program. It is nothing but a set of requirements for content development program. Each course/subject content development is treated as an individual project having a specific budget and timeline. This individual project further can be decomposed into content blocks and in turn content blocks can be decomposed into individual chapters or units.

3.4 Identifying the Content Development Projects

For each course, it is very rare that the content development program manager gets an individual subject expert for the entire course content development. It happens that a team can contribute for a single content development project. Also, the team members can be internal to the department, external to the department but within the organization and external to the department.

The unique characteristic of content development program is individual project domains are much diversified and it is difficult to identify the subject experts. However, the development process of a content development project can be repeated and reused. The first decision the program manager has to take for an individual project of content development is to decide whether to make or to buy.

3.5 Make or Buy Decisions

It depends on the program schedules and dependencies. If the project manager decides to develop the content within the organization, he has to deal with many resource related issues such as allocating office space, recruiting subject experts, arranging for meeting rooms, desk top facilities, and organising for library facilities (both online and offline). He has to draw an individual project plan within the framework of a program plan and kick off the project.

If the program manager decides to reuse the content from existing products in the organization, accordingly the individual project schedules have to be adjusted. If the program manager decides to buy the product from outside, he has to deal with vendors and content development companies.

Another model of content development is outsourcing. That is, the program manager decides to outsource certain blocks or units of the content to individuals outside the department (but within the organization), and individuals and companies outside the organization. Subsequently, the vendor management and relationship management play a major role. It is very difficult to continue the relationship with vendors keeping the low budget constraints.

3.6 Co-ordination between Different Projects

Once multiple stakeholders are involved, it is the challenge for the program manager to coordinate between different content development projects. Different individual projects may begin at different dates. However, the content development for the entire program has to be completed by the program completion date.

An object-oriented approach can be followed in content development. That is, *reuse* up to some extent is possible in content development projects. The components or sections can be reused across different content development projects. This saves a lot of time and money for the project and also the time of content research community is saved.

The main point of concentration is *coordination*. It is the best practice to allot a project coordinator or project manager for an individual project. It is the responsibility of the project coordinator to communicate with both internal and external subject experts, get the content, add value, integrate and deliver. Otherwise, it becomes unmanageable for the program manager to deal with 50+ internal and external subject matter experts. Based on the commonality in the content, the common components are to be searched or developed first for reuse purpose. Then, specific components are to be developed for the individual project.

3.7 Relationship Management with Vendors

The real people management and relationship building skills of the program manager come out in managing vendors in the industry. The program manager mostly looks for the ways to attract, retain, and motivate the talent in non-monetary ways. In current economic scenario and life styles, motivating individuals in this way is a major challenge. However, the program manager has to maintain professional relationship with both internal and external stakeholders such as subject matter experts, researchers, operations personnel, printing staff and learners. Relationship management is very much required in outsourcing model as well.

3.8 Challenges in Content Development Programs

Different content developers have different styles of writing. Getting a uniform structure for different units of the content development project from different content developers is a major challenge. One challenging area of review is the structural issues in the content. Other challenges include conceptual ambiguity, unwanted stressing of specific content and following the 80-20 rule. That is, one challenge is 80% of the content by the developer concentrates on 20% of the requirements. This rule should not be applied to content development. There should be uniformity across all topics in the requirements.

There may be many surprises to the program manager during execution such as the external experts dropping out of the program in the middle because of several reasons or their own tight timelines. It is also likely that the external subject expert is not good in the allotted area. However, he may be good in other areas which cannot be currently used.

The major challenge in the content development industry across the world is plagiarism. The program manager has to have his own set of tools and techniques to deal with it and improve the quality of content. The program manager has to maintain cordial relationship between content developers and reviewers. Other challenges are possible delays in the deliveries. Sometimes, the outside contributors are busy and they leave the content partially developed and then it becomes the responsibility of the project coordinator to fill the gaps.

3.9 Benefits and Value to the Stakeholders

The actual benefits of the program are achieved after satisfactory feedback from the learners. The program meeting, time, cost and quality parameters, satisfactory feedback from content developers, reviewers, operations team, program management team, and finally the learners are all attributes of a successful program. The return on investment can be in the form of increase in sales, repeat sales, and bulk sales of the content products.

It is very clear that program performance can be measured at any stage. This is not like software where product is not visible physically. The traditional program tracking and evaluation techniques can be applied to content development programs.

Program and project management are tools to implement an organizational strategy. The program manager has to have the skills of estimation, planning, decision-making, problem solving, negotiation and political skills. The program manager makes use of both internal and external resources in planning and executing the content development programs. Relationship management, continuous tracking, right decision-making, and right interventions are required in making content development program a success. This is possible through successful *project management*.

4

The Global Manager

For organizations that have established a mark for themselves in domestic markets, going international and then global are the next logical steps. According to a study conducted by The Economist Intelligence Unit in 2006, the overseas market will become more important for a majority of companies during the coming years. As a result, it is important for companies to reframe their strategy, structure, and managerial preparation to face the challenges of a global business entity.

The advancement in information and communications technology and the increasing degree of interconnection among markets implies that for any business to compete, having a global presence is essential. If companies do not take necessary steps to increase their scale and scope of operations, they may face the risk of being acquired. As a result of these factors, most organizations are facing the pressure of expanding their overseas operations.

4.1 What is a Global Organization?

The difference among domestic organizations, multinational organizations and global organizations is provided below:

1. **Domestic Organizations:** These organizations operate within the boundaries of the country from which they originate.
2. **Multinational Organizations:** These organizations establish business units which are similar to their domestic business in different parts of the world.
3. **Global Organizations:** These organizations are somewhat different from multinational organizations. They share and source resources on a global basis in order to provide

superior quality services and products at the lowest possible cost.

Global organizations differ from local organizations along the following four dimensions:

1. **Organizational Structure:** Within global organizations, the structure tends to be highly decentralized as compared to non-global organizations which have a high degree of centralization. Decentralization offers benefits such as tremendous flexibility and better customer relationships to a global company's operations in a particular country. However, the headquarters (HQ) play a vital role in integrating global authority. The HQ makes key decisions pertaining to strategy formulation. Certain functions such as IT, compliance and finance are controlled by the HQ.
2. **Management Processes:** As mentioned above, the headquarters play a vital role with respect to certain management functions. These functions are centralized and implemented through the HQ in order to achieve the organizational goals through a concerted effort. These functions include global strategy formulation, maintaining a global strategy information system, global budgeting, global knowledge sharing, cross-country co-ordination, global customer management, global performance review and compensation.
3. **Culture:** It is important for a global organization to integrate all its members through a global identity by having a global organizational philosophy and values that is communicated and reinforced across all units of the company. A global corporate culture is a worldwide system of shared values, behaviours and goals. For instance, Johnson & Johnson has its Credo in place. The Credo is a system of shared values. This serves as a binding agent which integrates all its employees together as a family.
4. **People:** The human resources of a global company comprises of employees from different nationalities, who follow multi-

country careers, and are required to travel frequently.

4.2 Categories of Global Managers

The role of managers is becoming more and more global in nature in the modern world. There are significant differences between a traditional manager and a global manager. The global manager needs a specific skill set in making the organization profitable and to achieve good customer satisfaction.

Global managers are categorized into three types. They are business managers, country heads and functional managers.

1. Business manager is termed as a strategist + architect + co-ordinator.
2. Country manager is termed as a sensor + builder + contributor.
3. Functional manager is termed as a scanner + cross-pollinator + champion.

Business managers should serve as strategists for their organizations, architects of its worldwide assets and resource configuration and the coordinators of transactions across national boundaries. The country manager should be a sensor of local opportunities and threats, the builder of local resources and capabilities, and contribute and actively participate in global strategy. Similarly, the functional manager must scan specialized information worldwide, "cross-pollinate" leading edge knowledge and best practices and champion innovations in the organization.

4.3 Nature of a Global Manager's Work

Global managers are business managers, functional managers and country heads. The business manager handles business profitability of a particular business. Either he heads a business unit or specific business operations of a global organization. Functional managers are working either as managers or heads of business functions such as marketing, human resources, finance, IT, engineering, production, and operations etc. Functional managers either work as managers within these departments or head these departments. Country managers head the organization in a specific country. They are responsible for the profit or loss of the business in that country. They do have the people responsibility most of the time.

For example, the country manager of a firm in India can become the head of the company for the Asia-Pacific region during his career. A country manager may expand his role to a wider region during his career span. With the globalization of businesses, country managers need to travel and meet with other country managers in order to explore and expand their business opportunities.

Business managers may be handling teams dispersed across the globe. They are responsible for teams spread across the globe. They need to travel to meet their customers, team members, suppliers and vendors. Similarly, if the organization is a global organization, even functional heads will have their teams spread across different countries. As a result, functional heads also need to travel to meet their teams abroad.

4.4 Skills Needed by a Global Manager

Global manager should have the stamina of an Olympic swimmer, the mental agility of an Einstein, the conversational skill of professor of languages, the detachment of a judge, the tact of a diplomat, and the perseverance of an Egyptian pyramid builder...And if he (she) is going to measure up to the demands of living and working in a foreign country, he (she) should have a feeling of culture; his (her) moral judgments should not be rigid; and he (she) should show no signs of prejudice.

A global manager is different from the traditional manager because a global manager has to manage teams across the globe in different countries with diversified cultural backgrounds. Nowadays, global managers are managing virtual teams as well.

These global managers need different skills in their day-to-day work. They are:

1. Customer focus skills
2. Communication skills
3. Leadership skills
4. Decision-making skills
5. Negotiation skills
6. Problem-solving skills
7. Mentoring skills
8. Interviewing skills
9. Presentation skills
10. Cross-cultural Skills
11. People management skills
12. Good listening skills

4.4.1 Customer Focus Skills: Customer is an important stakeholder for any project or business. The global manager is required to be in constant touch with the customers. According to a research done by DNL Global Inc., on international project teams, a global manager has to have customer focus skills in addition to the traditional managerial skills.

Usually, the global manager sends weekly status reports, contract agreements and billing information to the customer. Hence, the global manager needs to be able to negotiate billing and cost rates. He needs to negotiate on schedules and project deadlines as well with the customer. If the global manager lacks customer focus, it would be difficult to sustain the business.

4.4.2 Communication Skills: A global manager manages people while executing his work. He has the responsibility for managing people in the long-run. In his day-to-day activities, a global manager needs to communicate with his team members, customers, vendors, suppliers, senior management and partners. He has to communicate with all the stakeholders of business. According to a research done by Project Management Institute (PMI), USA, a project manager spends 90 percent of his time in communication. The modes of communication and media of communication may change. However, the need for communication in the global manager's job is very evident.

4.4.3 Leadership Skills: A global manager definitely needs to have leadership skills in leading the people, projects and businesses. Usually, global leaders exhibit different leadership styles in different situations. It is difficult for any global manager to sustain in the industry without leadership skills.

4.4.4 Decision-Making Skills: A global manager takes many decisions related to his project viz., technical decisions (in some cases), business-related decisions and people-related decisions. A global manager is responsible for the growth, reward and punishment of his team members. Hence, he needs to take many people-related decisions in his day-to-day work. Sometimes, he is responsible for the profit or loss of the business. Hence, he needs to take business-related decisions as well. A global manager has to take technical decisions if he is managing highly technical projects and technical people. This is very much true in the case of IT and telecom industries.

4.4.5 Negotiation Skills: A global manager communicates with team members, customers and vendors daily. He needs to negotiate about the cost, schedules, resources, and time lines with the team members. He needs to negotiate about billing rates and materials with the customer. He needs to negotiate the deliverables with the customer. A global manager needs to bargain with the suppliers and vendors to maximize profits.

4.4.6 Problem-Solving Skills: A global manager needs to have good problem-solving skills because, on a daily basis, he encounters problems, which needs to be solved using mathematical and scientific techniques. Hence, a global manager needs to have good problem-solving skills.

4.4.7 Mentoring Skills: Another responsibility of a global manager is to groom the successors in the business. For that, he needs to have good mentoring and coaching skills. Using his mentoring skills, he can mentor the young business executives in his department or in his line of career.

4.4.8 Interviewing Skills: A global manager participates in recruiting his team members and his subordinates. To recruit the right candidates, the global manager should have good interviewing skills. That is the reason all IT MNCs such as

Wipro, Infosys and TCS provide skills and training program to their projects, program and delivery managers.

4.4.9 Presentation Skills: At times, the global manager may have to visit the customer location for business purposes. During these visits, the global manager has to present his company to the customer. He may have to make a presentation about his company in seminars, conferences and trade shows globally. To do all these activities, the global manager needs to have the necessary presentation skills.

4.4.10 Cross-Cultural Skills: A global manager manages people from different countries with diversified cultural backgrounds. He has to be sensitive to cultural issues. The cultural issues are very important when interacting with cross-cultural teams.

4.4.11 People Management Skills: A global manager is responsible for his team members. He needs to set goals and objectives for his team members, evaluate and appraise their performance. The global manager has legitimate, referral, coercive, reward and expert powers to use among his team members.

4.4.12 Good Listening Skills: One should be a good listener first. Understanding comes with good listening. The communication between a speaker and listener becomes efficient with proper listening. Hence, when communicating with team members, other managers and customers, the global manager should use good listening skills for a fruitful communication.

4.5 Need for Orientation

Due to the widespread, complex and loose structure of a global organization, certain special efforts have to be made in order to integrate and bind all the units of the organization together. Ongoing training for global managers is essential.

Investing resources in developing global managers has assumed greater significance in recent times due to high degree of expatriate failure and need to manage overseas market efficiently. Managing overseas markets will become more important for a majority of companies in the coming years.

Managing in a foreign environment is not the same as managing within one's home country. A lot of managers who are sent overseas to handle foreign assignments have been unable to adjust to the foreign culture and environment as a result of which they have either performed poorly or returned before the completion of the assignment. Other reasons for their failure include inability of the manager's family to adjust to the new environment. The failure of a manager to perform his job as per the requirements of the assignment leads to substantial direct and indirect costs.

Direct costs include the manager's salary, foreign service premium, benefits, allowances, etc. which can be calculated. Indirect costs can be substantial too. They are invisible costs arising out of damage to customer relationships, relationships with other business partners, suppliers, local government, etc. Failure also leads to a loss of morale for the individual concerned as a result of which he (she) may find it difficult to adjust back in his home base.

In recent years, globalization has become a much more pressing issue. As a result, the skills of a global manager are in high demand.

4.6 Training and Development for Global Managers

4.6.1 Cultural Training: In order to obtain a first hand appreciation of the host country's culture, managers should be sent to the host country for a short visit. Field trips should be preceded by sensitivity training which includes an awareness of the values of the other culture; awareness of historical, political and economic information; comparison between home country and host country's culture; training on how to adjust to the other culture and how to cope with new situations without prejudice. It is also of vital importance for the manager to know how cultural factors will influence performance standards, participation and control, responsibility and authority, conflict and its resolution, attitudes towards task accomplishment etc.

4.6.2 Language Training: Learning the language of the host country can improve a global manager's productivity. Although English is spoken in several countries across the world, most countries also have at least one more dominant language which serves as the official language. Learning the language is especially useful if the manager is going to spend a long time in the host country. Speaking in the local language helps to encourage the employees in the local country, control the translator, and overcome difficulties in communication during business negotiations. Before imparting language training, a needs assessment has to be carried out to assess to what extent the manager will be expected to speak in the local language. Based on such an analysis, the level of competency to be achieved in the foreign language should also be assessed.

4.6.3 Practical Training: Practical training helps managers to adapt well to the external environment so that they can concentrate on their work. Adapting to local housing, transport, shopping, clothing, local school for the children, and other local facilities, are equally important. An awareness of these conditions helps the manager and the family members to quickly adapt to the local conditions of living. This enables to reduce the stress and concentrate on work.

To render the above training and developmental inputs, trainers can make effective use of methods such as role plays, simulations, case studies, experience sharing, films, lectures and books.

Global managers need to possess a myriad of skills to be successful. For global organizations, it is important to select the right people to work globally and to invest the right resources to groom and develop them. A global manager's job is becoming more and more complex day-by-day. Equipped with the skills outlined in this chapter, they should be able to deliver their commitments to the organization. Therefore, training and development assumes vital importance to ensure a global manager's success.

5

Conflicts in Top Management Teams (TMTs)

Conflict is multi-dimensional. Conflict is inevitable in organizations and it can be normal and healthy.

TMTs are required to solve complex and dynamic problems. They face ambiguous unstructured problems. TMTs make better decisions when more information is required and the problem is more ambiguous, unique and complex. TMT consists of the top two tiers in the organization including chairman, CEO, CFO, COO, and the next highest management tier.

TMT includes from inside board members till the vice-presidents. TMTs play a major role in strategy formulation, sales growth and organizational performance. The strategies and actions of CEO and his direct reports can make or break a company. TMT members manage from board of directors, to governmental officials, to shareholders, to analysts and partners. Decision-making in TMTs is multiparty and multi-motive negotiations. Participative safety is often low in TMTs. Usually conflicts in TMTs become public in the office which impacts the TMT climate.

5.1 Categories of Conflicts

Conflicts can be categorized as cognitive conflict, affective conflict and process conflict.

Cognitive conflict also known as task conflict is task-oriented and concentrates on common objective. Cognitive conflict involves differences of opinions, ideas and viewpoints.

Affective conflict, also known as relationship conflict, corresponds to individual incompatibilities, annoyance, tension, animosity, emotions, disputes, disaffections and interpersonal dislikes.

Cognitive conflict improves the decision quality. Affective

conflict reduces the decision quality, decision consensus and hampers the team performance.

Process conflict refers to the rules and procedures to be followed in accomplishing the task and roles and responsibilities in maximizing productivity. Team climate has to be managed to encourage cognitive conflict and discourage affective conflict.

5.2 Findings of Various Studies on Conflicts in TMTs

Studies on conflicts in TMTs have concentrated on demographic diversity such as age, education, functional diversity and tenure diversity. Some broad conclusions of these studies are as under:

1. Relationship between TMT team size, CEO dominance and organizational performance is significant when TMTs have high discretion in strategic decisions.
2. CEO dominance has adverse effects on decision quality because of lack of inputs from TMT members.
3. Conflicts occur at interdepartmental and interpersonal level mostly. Competition among individuals and departments are the main reasons for conflicts. The participants conveyed that the conflict is dysfunctional and destructive. The most favoured conflict resolution technique is the staff meeting. All the top executives believe that a conflict is dysfunctional and has negative consequences.
4. Functional diversity and educational diversity are negatively related to strategic consensus and tenure diversity is positively related to strategic consensus. Functional diversity is positively related to interpersonal conflict.
5. Relationship between task conflict and relationship conflict is mediated by the intra-group trust.
6. Impact of education, tenure diversity, and work experience on performance depends on the strategic and social context. There is a positive relationship between TMT education, functional diversity, tenure diversity and

performance and these relationships are stronger in short-tenured TMTs. TMT's situation affects the TMT demographic characteristics and outcomes. Demographic details impact TMT behaviour. Diversity is an advantage in most complex environments. The advantages with TMT heterogeneity are shared values, quick coordination and effective communication.

7. TMT cohesion is positively related to cognitive conflict and negatively related to affective conflict. TMT cohesion is positively related to new venture growth. Cohesive teams produce synergy, experience few process losses, experience fewer turnovers and tend to have longer tenures. Morale is positively related to belongingness and belongingness is negatively related to affective conflict.
8. Role of conflict in strategic decision-making is influenced by whether decisions are taken by team or individuals, informal behaviour and whether TMT members are following individual interests or organizational interests but not the individual or collective cultures.
9. National cultures can influence TMT decision-making. Individual interests and informal influencing are positively correlated to both cognitive and affective conflicts.

5.3 Reasons for Conflicts in Top Management Team

TMT size creates communication and coordination problems. The more the external contacts the more power is exhibited by the TMT members. The sources of TMT conflicts include data, interests, structures, values, and relationships.

Team problems come from its environment. Negative mood in team results into internal conflicts impacting team performance. TMTs having less cohesion tend to have more affective conflicts and experience higher turnover. Cognitive conflict turns into affective conflict in the presence of hurtful, harsh, forceful and aggressive tactics. Cognitive conflict can also turn into affective conflict in presence of raising voices. Cognitive conflict changes across issues whereas affective conflict is stable across issues.

5.4 Conflict Resolution Techniques

The most frequent conflict resolution techniques used by top management teams include avoidance, compromise, withdrawal, collaboration, confrontation and integration.

The best techniques to resolve conflicts in value differences, resources, structures and goal differences are the staff meetings and confrontation. Consensus is the best technique to resolve conflicts in value differences, attitude differences and poor communication. For dealing with conflicts in leaders having concern for others and concern for self with value differences, attitude differences and goal differences, the best conflict resolution techniques include avoidance, compromise and integration. Integration is the best technique to deal with conflicts because of resources and distribution of control in family businesses. Avoidance and collaboration are the best techniques to deal with resource conflicts.

5.5 Impact of Conflicts on TMT Performance

TMT performance measures include profitability, stakeholder opinion, slack resources and proximity to bankruptcy. Sales growth is another measure for new venture performance. Team leaders who exhibit emotional control tend to reduce affective conflict. Affective conflict is negatively related to sales growth and TMT performance. Cognitive conflict is beneficial to TMT performance. Cognitive conflict is less likely to convert into affective conflict in presence of intra-group trust. Conflict can stimulate participation from TMT members, and motivate and increase commitment from team members. Anxiety or frustration in TMT members over tough situations results in anger. Tenure diversity leads to low levels of conflicts and consensus and consensus is related to high levels of performance. Usually, conflicting TMT members fight for financial investments and losses, promotions to executive positions, executive compensation, unethical behaviour, and long range planning.

Positive mood among team members results in cooperation, less conflict, more participation and more social cohesion. The CEOs can be benefited by TMT functional diversity which can predict environmental ambiguity and reduce uncertainty. Selection and socialization among TMT members reduces conflicts resulting from demographic diversity. TMT members who feel belongingness are able to manage conflict better than those who feel less belonging in the team.

TMTs should manage the conflicts so that business relationships are maintained. Conflicts in TMTs can be managed using training, contingency planning, identifying vulnerabilities, what-if analysis, usage of planning tools, keeping everybody on same side of the table and crisis management through effective analysis of conflict situation.

6

Tata Group: A Case Study

6.1 Tata Group: History and Legacy

"Be it J.R.D. Tata or Ratan Tata. We always saw the Tata group as a rather different Indian enterprise, one that stood for decency, fairness, conscience, honesty, and even social transformation"—Ashwin Sanghi, (*Quartz India*, November 16, 2016).

Tata group is a multinational conglomerate based in Mumbai, India. Founded in 1868 by Jamshedji Tata, it gained global reputation for the series of foreign acquisitions it made over a long period of time. As of 2016, Tata group was into airlines, automotive, chemicals, financial services, software consulting, electrical distribution, engineering services, locomotives, consumer goods, steel, telecommunications, healthcare, real estate, defence and aerospace. Ratan Tata who hails from the Tata family was the chairman of the group between 1991 and 2012. Cyrus Mistry was the chairman of the group since 2012 till his ouster on October 24, 2016. Tata Group is a salt to software conglomerate.

Tata group (US$ 103.51 billion revenues in F.Y. 2016) employed around 6,60,800 persons across the world as in December 2016. As on September 13, 2016, 70 percent of the Tata group's revenues came from overseas businesses. They do business in all the five continents. They are the group which launched the cheapest car of the world 'Tata Nano' for ₹ 1,00,000 in 2008 via their venture Tata Motors.

Tata group has 29 publicly listed companies with combined market capitalization of US$ 120 billion. Tata Sons is the holding company of the group companies and Tata Trusts are the promoters having shares in Tata Sons. Tata Sons is not a publicly listed company. In addition to Tata Sons stake in group companies, one group company has stake in other group companies leading to a complex governing structure for the group.

6.2 Tata Group Performance

During Ratan Tata's regime between 1991 and 2012, group revenues grew at a compound annual growth rate (CAGR) of 19.2 percent. The group revenues grew phenomenally between 2001 and 2010 with major global acquisitions such as Corus and Jaguar Land Rover and big buyouts in beverages. However, Corus turned out to be a bitter experience with global economic meltdown in 2008. Ratan Tata's expansionist strategies increased group revenues from US$ 6 billion to US$ 100 billion in two decades along with acquiring major debt.

In September 2016, Cyrus Mistry, while speaking about corporate governance at Tata group opined, "keeping with Tata ethos, we are fully committed to maintain the highest standards of ethics and governance in the conduct of business by our enterprises".

On October 24, 2016, Mistry was supposed to present the corporate governance document before the board of Tata Sons in line with improving the corporate governance practices. On October 24, 2016, Mistry proposed corporate governance structure which clearly defined the role of board of directors of Tata Sons including reviewing of holding company's strategic plan periodically and reviewing the business plans yearly.

The business plan review included examining the cash flows, strategies, profit and loss, opportunities and risks along with approving the acquisitions and joint ventures in line with the government regulations. He also made similar plans for group companies along with defining the role of board of directors of Tata Sons. As on October, 2016, one of the major proposals of Mistry was to review the funding requirements of group companies.

Cyrus Mistry was in chairmanship of Tata group for nearly

four years from December 2012 till October 2016. On November 23, 2011, he was selected to be the vice chairman of the group to be groomed by Ratan Tata, and as his successor. Till December 2012, he was personally groomed and mentored by Ratan Tata. On December 28, 2012, he took over the Tata Group as its chairman with the retirement of Ratan Tata. Previously, Cyrus was part of the Tata's selection committee to lookout for a chairman. However, the selection committee selected him as their chairman. Mistry actually came to the Tata Group in 2006 as one of the directors of Tata Sons, after his father Pallonji Mistry's retirement from the board.

During Mistry's regime (2013-2016), Tata Group experienced compound annual growth rate (CARG) of 8.5 percent, which was half as compared to Ratan Tata's time CAGR. However, this lower growth rate was attributed to slowdown in China and global economic meltdown because of which Tata Steel and Tata Motors could not perform as expected. Mistry also attributed this slow growth rate to Ratan Tata era's of costly mistakes, which could not give enough freedom to act fast.

On September 13, 2016, Cyrus Mistry, Chairman, Tata Group, while talking about the speed and agility they were looking for their group of organizations said, "we are building the Tata Group of next 150 years". As on September 13, 2016, Mistry was optimistic about the Tata Group's future acquisitions both within and outside the country towards the organic growth of the Group.

As on October 2016, Tata Group was not happy with certain Mistry's decisions such as selling Tata Steel European unit.

As on November 19, 2016, TCS and Jaguar Land Rover businesses were generating significant profits and dividends for the group. However, the five businesses of the group such as motors, steel, power, hotels, and telecommunications arms were making them to lose money or not producing good returns over the cash invested. Tata's Nano car business was making losses too.

Mistry blamed Ratan Tata for some of the legacy issues the group faced and which were done during the tenure of Ratan Tata. According to Cyrus Mistry, Tata Nano project was a burden for the group; it was kept only for emotional reasons.

As on December 20, 2016, Mistry resigned from chairmanship of the six Tata Group companies and on December 21, 2016, he took legal route and filed a suit with National Company Law Tribunal (NCLT) against Tata Sons board and Tata Trusts. In the petition, he mentioned about the legacy hotspots such as Corus acquisition, Tata Nano car project, Docomo arbitration, and about Tata group investments in aviation sector. In the petition, he wanted NCLT to direct Tata Group not to dilute shareholding pattern in Tata Sons, which results in affecting his family firms, and not to remove Mistry as director of Tata Sons. He also mentioned in the petition that Tata Group mismanagement was affecting his family firms and his illegal removal from chairmanship seems like Tata group acting like a proprietorship firm, and directors of Tata Sons have failed to discharge their fiduciary duties.

On November 13, 2016, Tata Group called the shareholders meeting to vote to ouster Mistry from the chairmanship of Tata Motors, Tata Steel, TCS, Indian Hotels, and Tata Chemicals.

Part II
Project Management Research

7

Project Success Factors

Success of a project is concern for any industry. Because of the invisibility, complexity and flexibility of software projects, the success rate of software projects is just 32 percent. Hence, there is need for the study of project success and finding out the critical success factors. Project quality and project performance are related. Hence, we need to concentrate on the quality angle of the projects to make them successful. For the success of a project, organizations have to concentrate on team, project management, product, environmental, resources and technically related factors.

A product is known as a success if it product is widely used, there are very few defects, product is accessible, usable, compatible, portable and marketable. Based on different parameters or factors, one can say that the product is successful. Also in financial terms, if the return on investment is profitable to the organization and investors then only one can say that the product is successful.

7.1 What is Project Success?

The meaning of *project success* includes project success factors, project success criteria, project success measures, project success metrics and project success outcome evaluations. The presence of project success factors for project increases the probability of success of the project. Similarly, there are certain critical success factors for projects. The presence of these factors is mandatory for the success of the project. Project success can be measured using different techniques. Some organizations take customer satisfaction surveys. Some organizations take senior management or project manager feedback. Some organizations conduct project team surveys. Some measure the success of project in financial terms. They find out the cost deviance, schedule deviance and quality deviance of the project to measure the project success. Some organizations may take user ratings for the project.

Thus, different measures are used to check a project success.

7.2 Project Team

Project team factors impacting the success of the project include project coordinators and team members, their skills and competencies. Other team related factors impacting project success include team communication, team cooperation, team coordination, team cohesion, team conflicts, team climate, team productivity, and team performance. These factors impact the success of the project in any domain. These are all team processes impacting the success of a project. Team skills and competencies also have an impact on project success.

Similarly, team conflicts also impact the success of a project. Conflicts such as relationship conflicts, task conflicts, and process conflicts impact team cohesion. Team cohesion in turn impacts the team performance positively or negatively based on the type of conflict. The task conflict creating task cohesion is positively correlated to project success. The relationship conflict creating social cohesion is negatively correlated to the project success. The process conflict at the beginning of the project is good for the project and the process conflict at the end of the project can hamper the project progress. The project manager's behaviour also has impact on team processes and team behaviour. Team behaviour also impacts the project manager which in turn impacts the project success.

For project success, team factors such as conflict resolution, team cohesion, team climate, and team communication are the success mantras. Conflict resolution techniques used changes for different projects. The most widely used conflict resolution techniques include avoidance and compromise. Conflict resolution is also one of the success factors for projects. Similarly, team climate has impact on project productivity and performance.

7.3 Organizational Factors

Organizational factors impacting project success include organizational structure, reporting hierarchies, organizational strategy, organizational principles, procedures and policies, organizational culture, and organizational values. The CEO, top management behaviour, senior management commitment, organizational reputation, financial situation, customer relationship management, vendor relationship management, employee satisfaction levels, employee turnover, and attrition rates have impact on the success of a project.

Organizational factors such as reporting hierarchies, business processes, financial stability, internal and external environment like socio, politico, economic and legal factors also impact project success.

7.4 Technical Factors

Technical factors impacting project success include hardware factors, response times, access methods, speed of devices, accuracy of output, usability, accessibility, troubleshooting etc.

Technical factors such as machine return times, processing times, access times, troubleshooting, availability of technology, feasibility of implementation, cost of technology, commercialization of technology, technology transfer issues, understanding technology, availability of skilled manpower in that specific technology and training the team members on technology related products, etc. impact project success irrespective of the domain.

In case of software, mobile and digital technologies, hardware, software, firmware and middle ware technologies have an impact on project success. Innovation also impacts the technology factors in turn impacting the project success.

Even though technology is important, majority of the projects fail due to people related reasons. Hence, soft factors are to be carefully considered by the project team to make the project a success.

7.5 Environmental Factors

Environmental factors impacting a project success include external environment such as political, social, economic, legal, regulatory, and financial.

Environmental factors such as financial markets, stock exchanges, GDP, economic growth rate, fiscal situation in the country, financial reserves, relationship with banks and financial institutions, relationship with governmental regulatory bodies, political situation in the country, legal situation in the country, legal framework in foreign lands in case of international projects, expatriate payments, relocations, societal background of the organization, demographic background of the founders, etc. can also have an impact on project success.

7.6 Other Factors

Resources impacting project success are hardware, software, machinery, tools, and components used in project execution and planning. Project manager skills impacting project success include communication, leadership, persuasion, negotiation, influencing, motivating, directing, decision-making, problem-solving skills etc.

Research also indicates that educational background, age, demographic background such as geography, ethnicity, income levels, qualifications, and networking also have an impact on the financial success of organizations.

Innovation is also a distinguishing factor between a successful project and an unsuccessful project. Organizational culture, individual skills and creativity impact innovation in organizations. Innovation impacts project productivity and performance. Thus, innovation is also a success factor for projects.

Political, legal, cultural, technical, managerial, economic, environmental, social, and physical factors are critical factors for project management.

Research indicates that the top most success factors for a project include project objective or mission, top management commitment, competent project team and user involvement. Measuring project success in terms of cost, time and quality are the traditional approaches. The broad factors affecting project management success include project team, project resources, organizational environment, technical factors and project manager's skills.

Top management factors such as management commitment, management support, providing resources, quality orientation, and setting goals and objectives are also success factors for projects. Without top management support and dedication, a project may not be successful. This has to be there in all phases of the project. In the middle, if the top management drops their support, the project may not be successful.

Further, this research can be extended using empirical study to find out the impact of individual factors on project success. Statistical techniques such as correlation and regression can be used to find out the strength of relationship between dependent variables, that is, project success and independent variables. Project success can be measured in financial terms or stakeholder's perspective terms.

8

Critical Success Factors for Software Projects

8.1 Software Projects

A project has got special characteristics such as having a specific beginning date and an end date, specific goals, a set of complex interrelated tasks or activities and a limited budget. Organizations are transforming corporate strategy into actions using projects and project implementation. Usually, critical success factors can be used for project governance and communication in the project. These are the factors based on which project success is judged.

The success rate of software projects is still an area of concern in the world. Software development is complex and software developers are intelligent and deal daily with complex problems which in turn make the management formula in an organization complex. Project management research involves human, organizational, behavioural, environmental, cultural, contractual, legal, stakeholder, personality-based, communication and team-based factors and their interplay decides the outcome of a project.

Software product development is becoming global in nature because of shortage of skilled workers in a specific country and the pressure of time to market. When organizations go for global software development, they usually underestimate the impact of globally distributed software development teams and they need cooperation of culturally diversified teams. Executing international projects with different political, legal, social, cultural and infrastructural environments is more complex than executing projects in the domestic setup.

The success of software development project is an area of concern for many organizations in the world. The problem involves finding the critical success factors for software projects.

8.2 Software Projects are Different

According to Royal Academy of Engineering (2004), complex IT projects are an integral part of our society. Lack of constraints, invisibility, complexity and flexibility are some of the characteristics of complex IT projects. The level of professionalism observed in software engineering is lower than that of other branches of engineering, with some exceptions. Hence, with these complexities, executing software development projects and management of software projects are different from other engineering projects. Unlike other engineering disciplines, the same technical objective can be achieved in multiple ways in case of software engineering. Key players in software development include senior management, project manager, team members, system architects, users, vendors, suppliers, and customers.

Usage of computers and software has increased at an unprecedented rate. Computers are used at point-of-sale counters, ATM machines, electronic funds transfer, e-commerce, online purchases, online ticketing, online trading, financial accounting, automatic invoice processing and order processing. The volume of data, speed of response, and accuracy of expected results has made software projects more critical and complex. Accuracy, reliability, flexibility, accountability, reportability and completeness are some of the features of software systems. Once a software system is developed, it can be used any number of times. That is the reason why software projects are different from traditional projects.

Software development is a highly complicated work and involves many stakeholders. The success rate of software projects is not encouraging. Software development is done as projects and it involves knowledge from both software development and project management areas. Software projects are prone to have high risk because of changing requirements, different technical platforms, huge investments and different business domains. Software projects have multiple stakeholders. Each stakeholder has his or her own priorities and interests. Hence, software project success is an interesting area involving many facets.

8.3 Success Factors for Software Development Projects

Based on the exhaustive literature review of success factors for software projects, the following categories of success factors have been identified.

1. Communication factors.
2. Technical factors.
3. Organizational factors.
4. Environmental factors.
5. Product factors.
6. Team factors.
7. Project management factors.

These categories of success factors are also prioritized with respect to the success of software development projects.

8.3.1 Communication Factors: These are as under:

1. Communication.
2. Leadership.
3. Relationship between users and staff.
4. Reduced ambiguity.
5. Maximization of stability.
6. Balanced flexibility and rigidity.
7. Co-operation.

8.3.2 Technical Factors: These are listed as under:

1. Technical tasks.
2. Trouble shooting.
3. Technical uncertainty.
4. Technical implementation problems.
5. Integration of the system.
6. Technology support.
7. System testing.
8. Removing legacy systems.

8.3.3: Organizational Factors: These are as follows:

1. Top management support.
2. Realistic expectations.
3. Organizational politics.
4. Financial support.
5. Market intelligence.
6. Personnel recruitment.
7. Business process re-engineering.
8. Reducing cost base.
9. Increasing efficiency.

8.3.4 Environmental Factors: These are as under:

1. User involvement.
2. Customer involvement.
3. Vendor partnership.
4. External environment events.
5. Client acceptance.
6. User's confidence in the system.
7. Community involvement.
8. Legal problems.
9. User training and education.
10. Opening up a new market.

8.3.5 Product Factors: Following can be listed:

1. Accuracy of output.
2. Reliability of output.
3. Timeliness of output.
4. Quality control.
5. Documentation of systems and procedures.
6. Realization of user requirements.
7. Product management.

8.3.6 Team Factors: These are as under:

1. Team capability/competence.
2. Teamwork.
3. Selecting the right project team.
4. Project team coordination.
5. Task orientation.
6. Team commitment.
7. Team empowerment.

8.3.7 Project Management Factors: These are as follows:

1. Project planning.
2. Project control mechanisms.
3. Project schedule.
4. Availability of resources.
5. Project monitoring.
6. Project organization.
7. Project review and feedback.
8. Decision-making.
9. Problem solving.
10. Principles of earned value management.
11. Project selection.
12. Contractual arrangements.
13. Vendor package selection.
14. Evolutionary project management.

The practicing project managers can benefit from the identified critical success factors and categories of factors. With this, we can work towards the *ultimate goal of project management, making the project a success*. Further, an empirical study based on current conceptual model can further reduce the number of CSFs for software projects.

Further, an empirical research can be conducted based on the critical success factors (CSFs) identified for software projects so that top most CSFs can be identified. Similar approach and success factors can be found for projects in different industries such as construction, biotechnology, engineering, and pharmaceuticals. Finding out the critical success factors for different projects in different industries will increase the project success rate globally.

Further research can be done in finding the software projects' critical success factors specific to the delivery model the organizations are following such as onsite-offshore model, global delivery model, outsourcing and sub-contracting model.

The empirical research done on matured industries and on well established organizations and industries in finding out the critical success factors will definitely help the new entrants and start up organizations in that specific industry or country. If the findings of the critical success factors in different industries and in different countries can be well received, considered and implemented, the objective of *global project success* can be achieved by saving lot of valuable resources in this world.

9

Conflict Management Techniques in Projects

Conflict is an unavoidable component of human activity. According to one school of thought, conflicts are not good for projects. However, some scholars hold that conflicts are needed for better relationships and better performance in projects.

There has been a phenomenal increase in the interest on conflict resolution in recent times because of the increase in tensions namely, inter-personal, inter-group, inter-organization, and inter-cultural. Conflict management is a new entrant in the discipline of project management. Conflict is the most avoided part of project management.

9.1 Conflict Defined

Conflict is a disagreement between different parties over opinions, views and ideas. Moderate levels of conflict leads to better performance and high levels of conflict reduce team performance. Conflict may be the result of loyalty to something or attachment to something. Conflict may be a situation of parties in discrepancies, irreconcilable desires and incompatible wishes, activities, needs or goals.

Conflict is a phenomenon of experiencing negative emotional reactions by conflicting parties while pursuing their goals and perceived disagreements. The symptoms of conflict include jealousy, hostility, enforcing norms, regulations and rules, frustration and poor communication.

The three dimensions of an interpersonal conflict include interference, interdependence and disagreement. Currently, effective managers do not avoid conflicts but they take it as an opportunity for growth for both individuals and organization.

Sometimes, relationship conflicts lead to mistrust,

dissatisfaction, cynicism, apathy, non-cordial relationships, provoked hostility, anxiety and reduced project performance. The high level of conflicts also increases the costs and schedules of the project. Properly managed conflicts result in better quality product, better decision-making, greater innovation and enhanced performance.

Constructive conflict management comes along with mutual respect, cooperation and intention to learn from each other. Cross-cultural teams are prone to more conflicts. The seed of conflict is planted when one of the parties feels *disharmony* in projects. Traditionally, the word *conflict* has negative connotations.

Conflict involves struggle over claims such as resources, opinions, beliefs, status, desires, priorities, preferences and power. Existence of conflict depends on individual perception. When one party tries to impact the interests, objectives or goals of another party, the conflict exists.

9.2 Categories of Conflicts

Usually, conflicts in projects can be categorized as *cognitive conflicts* and *affective conflicts*. *Cognitive conflicts* deal with the differences in decisions and they are task-oriented. They are also known as *substantive conflicts*. *Affective conflicts* deal with differences in individuals and personalities and not on issues.

Conflicts can also be categorized as *functional conflicts* and *dysfunctional conflicts*. *Functional conflicts* are the constructive form of conflicts and *dysfunctional conflicts* are destructive to the team, organization or project.

Another categorization of conflicts pertain to *vertical conflicts,* which occurs between a superior and a sub-ordinate, and *horizontal conflicts,* which occurs between team members at the same level of hierarchy.

In projects, conflicts can occur between design and requirements, design and implementation and also among designers themselves. Construction projects are complex and different stakeholders have different conflicting interests and objectives. Usually, in the *storming* stage of team development, there are more chances of frequent conflicts.

9.3 Conflict Life Cycle

Conflict life cycle describes the dynamic nature of conflict comprising of different events or phases of the conflict in projects. This is called the *process model* of conflict, explaining the different internal events of conflict and their interaction. Conflict can be seen as a dynamic process rather than a static component or structure.

The four stages of a conflicting incident are as follows:

1. Antecedent conditions.
2. Cognition and personalization.
3. Behaviour.
4. Outcome (increased team performance or decreased team performance).

At the time of negotiations in the conflicting stage, the negotiation process has the following four steps:

1. Establish the issues and set the agenda.
2. Open moves.
3. Intensify negotiations.
4. Work out an agreement.

One can reduce stress, increase productivity and resolve challenges with the help of effective dialogues. Emotions play a critical role in conflicts and they have been understudied. Conflicts elicit emotions and emotions exist throughout the life cycle of a conflict.

9.4 Models of Conflict Management

Traditionally, conflict management models are of two types. They are *structural models* and *process models*. *Structural models* deal with factors impacting conflicts in projects and conflicting process. *Process models* deal with the sequence of events involved in the conflict. Process models are more dynamic in nature and structural models are more static in nature.

Initial models of conflict management were developed in 1970s by organizational and social psychologists. With respect to communication, there are three types of conflict management models. They are as under:

1. Integrative and distributive negotiation models concentrating on labour negotiations.
2. Mediation competency model concentrating on third party interventions.
3. Dual concern model concentrating on individual and informal conflict management in organizations.

The conflict management process has steps such as identify conflicts, analyse conflict, identify alternative solution, apply conflict resolution technique, choose the best alternative, implement the solution and review the impact.

The factors impacting the conflict management process are the personality differences, values, social and economic context and subjective individual and group preferences. Conflict management process also involves communication, power and persuasion. In the next section, the reasons for conflicts in projects are identified.

9.5 Identification of Reasons for Conflicts in Projects

There are many reasons for conflicts in projects. Table 9.1 lists top ten reasons for conflicts in projects.

Shared or common resources, differences in project goals or objectives are the top reasons for conflicts in projects. Interestingly, the leadership style of the project manager is not in the top ten reasons for conflicts in the project. Cultural and value differences are also the reasons for conflicts in projects.

9.6 Conflict Resolution Techniques

Structural conflicts can be resolved using procedural changes, personnel changes, resource changes, authority changes and layout changes. Inter-personal conflicts can be resolved using the conflict resolution techniques such as avoidance, give and take, problem solving, collaboration and negotiation.

Table 9.1: Top Ten Reasons for Conflicts in Projects

Serial Number	Reason for Conflict	Number of Occurrences in Literature
1.	Shared/common resources	14
2.	Differences in project goals/objectives	12
3.	Cultural differences	10
4.	Value differences	10
5.	Personality issues	10
6.	Differences in technical opinions/approaches	9
7.	Schedules	9
8.	Costs	8
9.	Administrative procedures	8
10.	Different perceptions	7

Asserting ensures win for one party at the expense of other party. It is a one way solution. *Domination* and *forcing* creates win-lose situation for all the parties in conflict.

Integrating style is an effective approach for project performance and it creates a win-win situation for the parties. *Avoiding* is most disruptive style of conflict management in projects. In this style of conflict resolution, one party is indifferent to feelings of other party and one party keeps away from participating in conflict at all. It leaves the conflict unresolved and creates anger or frustration in other party and propagates the conflict further.

In *accommodating*, one party sacrifices their own needs, wants and expectations to satisfy the other party. In *compromising* style of conflict resolution, both the parties give and take and they win something and lose something. *Confrontation* or *problem solving* tries to satisfy all the parties in conflict by keeping all the facts and figures in picture and using scientific techniques in solving the problem. It creates a win-win situation for all the parties in conflict. Understanding each parties standing through a pre-caucus is a foundation of conflict management.

One defensive approach is to change the topic. *Smoothing* technique results in lose-lose situation for both the parties. It does not provide a permanent solution to the conflict but it provides a temporary fix. *Forcing* creates a win-lose situation. The forcing party wins and the other party loses. But it does not provide a positive impact over the long-run. *Negotiation* is a process of interaction between both the parties using different communication channels in resolving conflict in a mutually beneficial way. *Collaborating* and *accommodating* are the cooperative styles of conflict resolution and *avoiding* and *competing* are uncooperative styles of conflict resolution. *Collaboration* in an attempt to satisfy all the parties creates a win-win situation for all the parties. It is the most valued strategy in the industry.

Also, *competing* and *collaborating* are assertive styles and *avoiding* and *accommodating* are unassertive styles of conflict resolution. Using *collaboration,* one can create a win-win situation for the parties in conflict. *Authoritative command* is different from *forcing* because authoritative commands can only be given by the project manager; whereas, forcing (in different means) can be done by any team member or any other stakeholder.

Cooperative styles of conflict resolution create positive emotions in the team, leading to constructive conflict management and in turn resulting in better relationships, performance, organizational environment, and innovations.

Top management in organizations need *integration* style of conflict resolution. This style is positively associated with team performance. Cooperative conflict resolution styles such as *integrating, accommodation* and *compromise* are positively associated with higher levels of constructive conflicts, lower levels of destructive conflicts and increased innovations and performance. Non-cooperative and competitive conflict resolution strategies such as *avoiding* and *forcing* are negatively related to constructive conflicts and increase destructive conflicts leading to reduced innovations and performance.

Compromise is not effective at project level but it may be good at the organization level. Collaborating is positively related to team performance and compromising is negatively related to team performance. While dealing with conflicts, one has to avoid tit-for-tat reactions in organizations.

While dealing with conflicts, the managers have to separate people from the conflict and have to concentrate on the issues not on the positions. The project manager who deals with fairness is respected much by the team members in the long-run. The specific conflict resolution technique has to be chosen based on the importance and type of conflict, time pressures, emphasis on task vs. relationships, and the position of the members involved in the conflict. The important point in resolving conflict is that one has to balance between adjusting self and adjusting others.

Table 9.2 presents top five conflict resolution techniques in projects as available in the literature on the subject.

Table 9.2: Top Five Conflict Resolution Techniques in Projects

Serial Number	Conflict Resolution Technique	Number of Occurrences in Literature
1.	Avoiding/withdrawal	27
2.	Compromising	26
3.	Confronting/problem solving	17
4.	Accommodating	13
5.	Smoothing	13

People use avoiding and compromising more frequently than any other conflict resolution technique; followed by confronting, accommodating and smoothing. How to analyse a conflict is given in the next section.

9.7 Conflict Analysis

Conflict analysis should be done with self-introspection

and estimating the cost of conflict. Inter-personal conflicts can also be analysed using transaction analysis. It is the best practice to prioritise the conflicts when multiple conflicts are present in the project. Conflict analysis includes brainstorming to discover the present and future conflicts, cluster related conflicts, prioritize conflicts with 'urgency' and 'significance', identify the important conflicts and also identify the stakeholders related to the conflicts.

The project managers have to listen carefully to the team members and attitude, communication and negotiations are keys to conflict management. *Cognitive conflict analysis* approach involves the following six steps:

1. Identification of conflict.
2. Generation of conflict cases.
3. Judgement execution.
4. Results analysis.
5. Cognitive feedback.
6. Negotiations between conflicting parties.

9.8 Choosing the Best Alternative

Conflict has got both positive and negative outcomes. Positive outcomes include innovations, creativity, greater self-awareness and learning. Negative outcomes include competition, disputes, strained relationships, low morale, inefficiency, low productivity and performance, grievances, attrition, higher absenteeism, mistrust, low motivation and less job satisfaction and reduced coordination and cohesiveness. Usually, project managers prefer negotiations to find the best alternative solution for the conflict in picture. The attitude of project manager is a predictor of conflict outcome. When the project manager exhibits a positive attitude, more beneficial outcomes result from the negotiation process. In conflicting situation, one has to convert the destructive conflict into a constructive cooperation and collaboration for better project performance.

It is the style of conflict resolution and which technique is used in conflict resolution that determines the positive or negative outcomes. Hence, based on the outcomes of conflict resolution, one has to decide the best alternative solution for conflict in picture. In information systems development, satisfactory conflict resolution has got positive impact on information systems outcomes. *Partnering* is one of the conflict prevention method used in large scale urban projects in Canada.

Most of the research on conflict management has concentrated on conflict resolution rather than on conflict prevention. The advantages of partnering include increased team work, new opportunities, fostering team spirit, clarified communication and decision-making processes. Choosing the best conflict resolution style is the most fundamental skill for project managers.

9.9 Review the Impact

The impact of conflict and its solution implementation can impact at individual, team, project, business unit and organizational level. The impact on individual will be in terms of job satisfaction and individual performance. The outcomes or impact on project include project success with impacting dimensions such as schedules, costs, quality, specifications and process satisfaction. The impact on team would be increased or decreased innovation, productivity, and performance. The impact on organization would be in terms of organizational efficiency, effectiveness and performance. The organizational and business unit earnings and profitability can also be impacted by the conflict management in projects. Thus, the project manager and top management should review the above mentioned dimensions after implementing the solution to the conflict in picture. Task conflicts play a major role in innovations, decision quality, creativity and in generating new ideas and thoughts.

Implementation of solution for conflict may result in additional costs as well. The conflicts and styles of conflict resolution in projects affect individual, team, project, departmental and organizational outcomes. Sometimes, they even impact the country's economy at large if it is a huge project. The project manager needs to handle the conflicts in such a fashion so as to reach at a constructive functional conflict using techniques such as communication, heterogeneity and competition.

It is the best practice to have a conflict management plan with strategies to handle conflicts whether to prevent, resolve, prioritize or act. It should also consist of capacity building and training steps and measures to deal with conflicts. Large team size, functional diversity and team tenure diversity promotes constructive conflicts in projects.

10

Project Management Insights from *Bhagavad Gita*

In the modern world, employee confidence, assertiveness, job satisfaction and work-life balance are very much important for global organizations. There is evidence of organizations using *Bhagavad Gita* to achieve these objectives. These are not the only applications of *Bhagavad Gita*. It can also give insights on project management.

10.1 About Bhagavad Gita

Bhagavad Gita is the essence of all *Puranas*. It is very simple and assertive. Every word in Bhagavad Gita is taught in a positive attitude and positive essence. Bhagavad Gita consists of 18 chapters known as *adhyayas.* It consists of 700 *slokas* written in Sanskrit. The broader context of Bhagavad Gita is the epic *Mahabharata.* Bhagavad Gita was narrated by Lord Krishna to Arjuna and was watched by Sanjaya with the *divyadrishti* given by the Veda Vyasa. Bhagavad Gita as part of Mahabharata was scripted by Veda Vyasa. Researchers express that it was scripted between 2nd and 5th century BC. There are different perspectives or claims over the date of authorship of Bhagavad Gita.

Bhagavad Gita talks more about project strategies, project leadership, individual characteristics, and project culture. The broader project context and environment can be found from the Mahabharata. There have been many scholars who brought management effectiveness, strategy and leadership insights from Bhagavad Gita in the literature.

According to my knowledge and search on Google and Google Scholar, till now, none of the researchers or practitioners has tried to bring the project management insights from the ancient Bhagavad Gita. This is my journey towards the exploration of Bhagavad Gita seeking the insights for the growing and emerging discipline of project management.

In broad, Bhagavad Gita gives more about individual values, behaviour and capabilities and leadership qualities required for project performance, success and effectiveness.

To express the *Kauravas* as enemies of *Pandavas*, the word "competitors" was used which docs have a business sense too. These insights are useful not only in the Indian context, but also in the global context as more research and exploration was carried out on Bhagavad Gita in the Western world as well. Many global corporations and MNCs are looking for ways to improve employee work-life balance, self-confidence, assertiveness, job satisfaction, loyalty, personality development, ethics and commitment using Bhagavad Gita. This is very much applicable in a dynamically changing global economic and business scenario.

10.2 Project Stakeholders

The important stakeholders mentioned in Bhagavad Gita are Lord Krishna, Arjuna, Pandavas, Kauravas, Dhritarastra, Sanjaya, Bheeshmacharya, Vidura, Guru Dronacharya, Vyasa, Duryodhana, Dhrishtadyumna, and Maharshi Narada.

Some of the characteristics of ideal stakeholders as discussed in Bhagavad Gita are discussed here also. In Bhagavad Gita, Lord Krishna likes people who do not discriminate, who do not hate, who like all the creatures of the world, who has mercy, who treats happiness or sadness equally, who believes in equality, which has control over his body and mind, who has control of his senses and who has a deterministic mind. Similarly, customers also like these kind of people in current business scenario. Customers also like individuals who do not make others worry, who do not get influenced by others and who do not have fear, jealousy and aggression as Lord Krishna liked.

Lord Krishna also likes one who executes the task,

maintains physical and mental neatness, one who does not have dangerous desires, who is not biased and one who does not get influenced by unhappiness. One should have equal feeling about friends, enemies and competitors. Other characteristics of stakeholders include purity, non-violence, egoless, polite talk, respect for individuals, control of senses, consideration for birth, death and ill-health and external and internal neatness.

Nature has created three characteristics in human beings. They are *sattva, raja*, and *tama*. These are known as *trigunas. Sattva* is the ideal one. The people with *sattva* characteristics do peaceful tasks which gives happiness. This binds human beings with happiness and knowledge. People with *raja* characteristics do tasks with *kama* and curiosity. This binds the individuals in executing tasks all the time. People with *tama* characteristic do tasks which attract their body and non-knowledgeable things. This binds the individuals with dangerous things and sleep.

If you control, *raja* and *tama* characteristics, *sattva* pops up. If you control *sattva* and *raja* characteristics, *tama* pops up. If you control *sattva* and *tama* characteristics, *raja* pops up. These three characteristics of individuals are interrelated.

With the activation of internal body senses and consciousness, *sattva* characteristics increase in an individual. *Raja* characteristic leads to lust, curiosity, expectation of benefits, and worrying attitude about others things. When the *tama* characteristic increases, an individual loses sense of body and mind, drifts away from tasks, does unproductive things, and engages in dangerous acts. By executing ideal tasks, one gets happiness, knowledge and *vairagya* (detachment).

Execution of tasks with *raja* characteristic leads to sadness. Execution of tasks with *tama* characteristic leads to foolishness. *Sattva* leads to knowledge, *raja* leads to lust, and *tama* leads to dangers. *Sattva, raja* and *tama* characteristics happen automatically and go away automatically for an ideal person. They are not constant for an ideal person. An ideal person won't worry when they get away on their own. An ideal person has to be away from *trigunas.*

According to Bhagavad Gita, the *family culture* has got strong roots in the society. There is no beginning (*aadi)* and end (*antam)* for the family tree. A *gyani* can only know about their self when they are enjoying the benefits of information, full of *trigunas,* and they are stable minded. *Agnani* cannot be aware of self. The *divine qualities* of a stakeholder include non-violence, truth, non-anger (helping even the enemies), sacrifice, peace, mercy, excuse, courage, non-enmity, not blaming others, and not doing useless things.

The *ghost qualities* include anger, cunningness, ego, pride, harshness and foolishness. Stakeholders have either divine qualities or ghost qualities. Stakeholders with ghost qualities do not talk about the truth, do not consider the tasks in hand, have no ideal behaviour and lack cleanliness. They think that it is only the *kama* which is creating things in the world. They will be worrying till the end and are obsessed with the returns and benefits.

They follow *adharma or* unlawful/unethical roots to make money. They think that they can finish the competitors and are the strongest. A stakeholder should be away from *kama* (desire), *krodha* (anger) and *lobha* (greed).

According to Bhagavad Gita, every human being has some interests and accordingly executes the tasks based on his interests. Meditation is a good method for individuals to attain peace of mind and remain calm.

10.3 Project Management Concepts and Framework from *Bhagavad Gita*

Project management concepts such as project strategies, project planning, individual task, individual (team member), project leader, project execution, and motivation can be derived from Bhagavad Gita. The characteristics, qualities, impacts, effects, and applications of these concepts are discussed in Bhagavad Gita. These have to be looked from a micro point of view through the 700 slokas of 18 chapters in Bhagavad Gita. Next section describes the project management framework derived from Bhagavad Gita.

A project management framework consists of components such as individual behaviour, project strategy, project leadership, team work, project culture (values), team skills and capabilities, and project planning. More about project environment and project plan can be found in the epic *Mahabharata*. This section brings more insights on project stakeholders, task characteristics, project execution, project leader and team member characteristics and behaviour. The focus is to explore *human resources management* as a knowledge area.

In the 7th chapter of Bhagavad Gita, Lord Krishna told Arjuna that *nature* is of 8 different types. These are earth, water, fire, air, sky, mind, heart and ego. We use all these as resources for our projects whether it is construction, software, biotechnology, pharmaceutical or any engineering project. *Nature* and *human resources* are very ancient. The *characteristics* of nature include creation of love, hate and material resources. Nature can create projects and tasks. The *characteristics* or *peculiarity* of individuals in projects include decision-making capability, knowledge, being away from desires, truth, control of *pancha indriyas*, control of mind, creativity, fear, equality, meditation, reputation, and respect. All these are the result of *karma* of an individual. These are the by-products of task execution in a project. One can execute the projects and tasks by knowing the characteristics of *nature* and *individuals*.

Team members get the feel of happiness or unhappiness in the project through *communication*. They exchange ideas, views and opinions with respect to the project. Discussions are common for decision-making in projects. Qualities of *purushottama* include creation, knowledge, wealth, strength, and courage. These qualities are evident in senior management in some of the organizations even in current days.

According to Bhagavad Gita, Lord Krishna suggested Arjuna to have *abhyasa yoga,* that is, training required to execute a project. This is applicable to project leaders as well. The project leaders have to undergo training and practice the same by keeping the mind in control. Knowledge is more important than the training without knowing the meaning. Experience is more important than the knowledge. Results are more important than the experience. Similarly, project results and benefits are more important than the project team experience. Donating the project results is more *sacred.* This gives peace of mind to the project stakeholders. Next section explains the individual task characteristics as extracted from Bhagavad Gita.

10.4 Task Characteristics

Bhagavad Gita assigns tasks to individuals basis their *caste*. In project management, the task is assigned based on the skill set or role of team members. In project management, customer is the creator of tasks. In Bhagavad Gita, God is the creator of tasks. Thus, the industry saying "customer is god" is justified. According to Bhagavad Gita, task is nothing but *karma.* Entire project team should have task orientation or *karma* orientation for project success. One should not have anxiety over the result of *karma*. Project team members having control over senses, mind and who are away from materialistic things with stable mind can perform the tasks well. Project team members having equal opinion about happiness or unhappiness, satisfaction, non-jealousy, balanced feeling for stability or instability, and certainty or uncertainty can perform the tasks well.

According to Bhagavad Gita, all tasks end with creation of *knowledge*. Project team members with equality towards stakeholders should proceed to execute the tasks. In Bhagavad Gita, Lord Krishna told that instead of going away from tasks, it is better to pursue the tasks for good. The members who are away from personal attachments, desires and hate can perform the tasks well.

An individual who has self-control over his mind, *pancha indriyas*, and believes in equality among all creatures can execute difficult tasks more comfortably. Those tasks would not impact him personally. A person, who is listening, understanding, seeing, eating, watching, hearing, walking, sleeping, smelling, talking, deserting, and opening eyes, thinks that his *indriyas* are doing the tasks but he is not doing any task. A *karma yogi* performs the tasks by keeping his mind, body, and senses under control for his internal cleanliness. Such people gain peace of mind.

A member, who worries much about the incentives of the task execution (*karma phal apeksha)* all the time, does not find peace in his mind. Mostly, the personality and personal characteristics only decide the results of *karma.* An individual who executes the tasks without expecting returns or benefits is a *yogi.* In this materialistic world, it is difficult to retain this quality. At the same time, an individual who goes away from tasks, or who deserts the tasks is not a *yogi.* An individual who executes the tasks without a desire (*kama*) can become a *yogi.*

According to Bhagavad Gita, every task (*karma*) has beginning (*aadi*) and end (*antam*). This is the characteristic we are highlighting for project or task in modern day project management. Individuals who are away from sins, who have clarified their doubts through knowledge, who seek well-being of all creatures and who have stable mind, can perform the project tasks well. They are best suited as human resources for project execution. One has to satisfy himself more or so because one is friend of his own or an enemy of his own. An individual who has gained control over his body, mind and *indriyas* is his own friend. The one who does not win over them is his own enemy.

Actually, body, mind and *indriyas* help an individual, if he wants to gain control over them. Otherwise, they will become enemies of an individual and won't allow him to reach the project goal. They can become constraints or show stoppers to reach the goal. Next section highlights the project execution aspect from Bhagavad Gita.

10.5 Project Execution

The project in Bhagavad Gita was the *war* between Pandavas and Kauravas. The project location was *Kurukshetra*, the place of war. A sub-project plan was written in the form of *padmavyuham,* by Kaurvas. Dhrishtadyumna was also involved in framing strategies for the Pandavas. Duryodhana was worried about the team capabilities and competencies of Pandavas. The project was kicked-off with fearful sounds of instruments at the battle ground by Kauravas. Pandavas kicked-off the work with Lord Krishna's divine *shanka*.

Bhagavad Gita says do not worry whether you win or your competitor wins, before executing the project. Just execute the project for the benefits and leave the rest to God. One should not have a competitor cantered or enemy cantered mindset all the time. One should not worry much about the weather seasons such as winters, summers, autumn or spring to execute a project. Irrespective of the season, the project execution should continue. The project team should not worry much about the uncertainties, risks and unknowns. They should plan for them. The project leader should not fear for execution of the project and organizational tasks and responsibilities. He has to act ethically.

If the project leader expresses his inability to execute a project, the senior management takes him easy. His opponents and competitors would criticize him. In the 8th chapter of Bhagavad Gita, Lord Krishna told to Arjuna to have control over body and senses and concentrate on project execution. Lord Krishna told Arjuna to have a stable mind, control over *pancha indriyas* and keep mind on heart with stability and continue executing the project. Here, Lord Krishna suggested considering the opinion of heart instead of brain. In current day project management, we use quicker decisions utilizing brain rather than the heart because of the dynamically changing business conditions and increased stress levels.

Unproven assumptions are not good for project success. To get expertise in any task, team members have to work with determination, patience and interest. Practice brings expertise in a task. One has to work with courage and intelligence. Unstable mind always thinks about the outer world things. One has to control and without deviating mind they have to put effort towards project execution. A patient individual without interest at materialistic things and having concentration towards work can gain ultimate happiness in work. Team members who are capable and look at all the natural things equally treat all the creatures equally with stable mind. Individuals doing day-to-day tasks to run their families and self-fulfilment can never be destroyed. An individual who tries and practices for excellence can reach greater heights.

According to Bhagavad Gita, knowledge-based education is the ultimate education one can give to team members. This is more easy, successful and practical. In Bhagavad Gita, Lord Krishna creates all the creatures in the world, nothing but just like the current day product creation. He creates and destroys the products, which is applicable till date. Nobody knows how he created the products. In other words, it means maintaining trade secrets in today's world and retaining intellectual property. The work done with pure mind without desires is liked by God and in modern days by the organizations. The project leader (or project manager is used in synonymous terms) characteristics are explained in the next section.

10.6 Project Leader Characteristics

Bhagavad Gita talks about the individual and internal discipline the project leader should have. According to Bhagavad Gita, the project leader expressed his inability to execute the project in the beginning. The project leader was scared to execute the project by looking at the competitors. It was because of the consequences, outcomes, and results which may have impacted some stakeholders negatively. However, with able coaching by Lord Krishna, he gained courage, assertiveness, empowerment and enlightenment required to execute the project.

By seeing the complexity of the project to be executed, the leader's behaviour, mental and physical attributes were immediately impacted. Because of the project complexity and stress, the project leader was not even able to stand properly. This is very much applicable in today's times as well. The project leader of Pandavas, Arjuna lost his courageous son Abhimanyu on the 13th day of the war. Still, he continued the project work and showed his commitment and dedication. A team leader should trust his team, their skills and capabilities. The project leader may be denied the incentives, perks and benefits he is going to get after the project completion in the beginning itself. This indicates the complexity of the project. As in Bhagavad Gita, before project execution, the project leader's eye became wet and he almost cried while executing the project. However, to gain reputation and recognition, the leader came back. Similarly, in the modern day connotation, in need of the hour, a project leader should not disappear or desert the place.

Project leader should not be cowardice. At some stage, the project leader was not interested to have all the benefits accruing to him without sharing with his team members. The project leader has to decide it being ethical or unethical. That is, *dharma* or *adharma*. A leader cannot sustain in a leadership role with unethical practices. A project leader should not worry too much at personal level about the existing team members or the ones who have left the team. A project leader should have equal feelings about happy and unhappy movements. He should not be worried much for unhappy things and feel very excited for happy things. This is because, according to Bhagavad Gita, every task involves some problems, risks or uncertainty. Every task leads to creation of knowledge useful for the project and the organization. It extends learning to an organization. There is no question of inability in the task execution.

Bhagavad Gita suggests against unnecessary luxuries, lavish parties and entertainment. Here, the keyword is *unnecessary*. Duryodhana underestimated the enemy's or competitor's capabilities. Bhagavad Gita expresses that project leader should not have personal attachment with the team. However, he should respect and guide them in project execution. A project leader should be away from personal attachments while monitoring and executing the project. In Bhagavad Gita, Arjuna was stepping back to fire his own people, which is also required in current day's continuously changing business conditions, mergers, acquisitions and partnerships.

If a project leader does not execute the project towards success, he loses recognition and respect. Stakeholders and the team may talk about him in an unrespectable way impacting his reputation. The team thinks that he left the organization because of his inabilities. Even if competitors and colleagues criticize, the project leader should not stop from leading the project. If he wins the project, he and his team gains the benefits, if he loses the project, still, there is some learning for the individual and the organization. So, the project leader should have the commitment, determination and courage in leading the team.

The current day project management requires stopping the project if it is unprofitable for an organization. Unless they have other reputational issues, the organization won't continue with the unprofitable project. An individual who takes away all the project benefits without sharing may not be a good project leader. Project leader should be unbiased towards his team members. Even if the project leader collects different opinions, final decision should be taken keeping values and ethics in picture. *Self dharma is more important than para dharma.* Following *para dharma* is more dangerous. A project leader should not get influenced by others in his key decision-making.

Satpurusha is the one with a deterministic mind. He cares about others more than himself. He does ethical business. His mind is always peaceful. In Bhagavad Gita, a project leader has the power of meditation. In chapter 11 of Bhagavad Gita, Lord Krishna presented Arjuna with *divyadrishti.* It is nothing but the ultimate or divine *vision*. Using vision, the project leader can do short-term and long-term planning, projections and estimations. Vision is very much required for project planning and execution.

By seeing the *visvarupa* of Lord Krishna, there was a change in Arjuna's braveness, courage and peace of mind. After showing his *visvarupa*, Lord Krishna told Arjuna that even if he won't participate in the war, none of the competitors will remain. Hence, instead of going away from the project (war), execute the project. Hence, to gain *keerthi,* reputation, fame, name, wealth and position, the project leader should execute the project.

In *visvarupasandarshana yoga*, Arjuna respected Lord Krishna both from front and back. This should be true in case of respecting customer and stakeholders as well in project management. Arjuna asked for excuse from Lord Krishna for his mistakes and underestimating the Lord.

10.7 Individual (Team Member) Behaviour

According to Bhagavad Gita, individual skills, competencies and knowledge are important for project execution. This is evident from Duryodhana's confidence in his team capabilities. It expresses not to cheat fellow colleagues and other team members. There should be trust in the team. Bhagavad Gita denies *unethical* practices. It talks about respecting each individual's religion, race, language and gender. It talks about respecting the senior and top management. Bhagavad Gita expresses that one should not go walk away from his skills and competencies. One should not desert his tools and techniques.

According to Bhagavad Gita, one will look at things

curiously. One will talk about it curiously. One will execute it curiously. A project team should not leave the unexpected or new opportunities coming their way. Entertaining individuals all the time should not go behind the unnecessary desires and wants. This is because, according to economics, human needs are unlimited. One should not have much curiosity about the future individual benefits. One has to have control over his body and its senses. Every individual contribution is significant in team work. An individual should have control over his work but not on the result.

Team members should continue the work and results follow. Instead of having curiosity over the results, team members should concentrate on their assigned tasks. One has to have equal feeling about being stable or unstable, and in certain or uncertain situations. Individuals who keep the future incentives in mind all the time, won't be able to give their 100 percent at work.

One should not have greed and lust. Even if the team member receives different opinions from various stakeholders, he has to think twice and take a decision. Self-satisfied person always performs better in projects. An individual who does not worry for sorrows, who does not feel over joyous in happiness, who does not have too much curiosity and who is away from fear and anger is known as *Sthitaprajna.* An individual having control over *pancha indriyas*, that is, having control over the senses of five organs namely, eyes, ears, skin, tongue, and nose (see, hear, touch, taste, smell) would have a stable mind. *Sthitaprajna* cannot be affected because of benefits and incentives.

Curiosity leads to desires in human beings. If desire is not fulfilled, it leads to anger. Anger leads to senselessness. Senselessness leads to disasters and degrade in an individual's personal and professional life. Thus, an individual having control over his senses would have peace of mind. A calm and relaxed individual with peace of mind can perform well in project execution. An individual not having control over mind and senses won't be able to take stable decisions. He won't find interest over something or he won't find happiness in life. Thus, an individual having control over his body and senses can take stable decisions.

An individual who is away from egos and personal attachments can find peace of mind. Team members should not go away from tasks assigned to them. A best individual is one, who keeps his mind and senses under control and executes the assigned tasks. If an individual does not perform tasks or goes away from tasks, his body won't be under his control. Maintaining his body and senses become difficult.

Team members get into trouble by executing the tasks which were not assigned to them. Team members who work without selfishness and cooperate with each other can have mutual satisfaction in project. A team member who does not execute the assigned tasks and fulfils desires of all his *pancha indriyas* is not the right fit for the project. Team members should execute the tasks without any anxiety. A *gyani* performs the tasks without anxiety, with his natural behaviour by keeping his mind in control. *Agnani* performs the tasks with anxiety. An individual with ego thinks that he is the creator of tasks.

Love and *hate* are the most dangerous things in the world for any individual. They can help an individual's growth or they can destroy an individual. Because of hate and love, people get into happy or unhappy situations. Desire, in other words *kamam,* leads to anger in an individual. *Gyani's* knowledge is covered with *kamam* just like dust over mirror, and smoke over fire. *Kamam* is like fire. It is overshadowing the knowledge. To control the *kamam*, one has to have control over senses first.

Mind is more important than pancha indriyas. Having sense is more important than mind. Soul is more important than sense. Thus, one has to remove kamam by having control of five senses. *Gyani* achieves self-control by controlling his five senses. With this, they can concentrate on their tasks, even in case of disturbances such as sound and human presence.

Because *agynanam* is overshadowing the *gynanam* (ultimate knowledge), people tend to get attracted to each other. *Gyani* has equal feelings about *Brahmin, elephant, cow, dog* and unwise people. A gyani having equality among all the things can think out of the box. A team member who controls his *kama* (desire) and *krodha* (anger) even while in the team is the real happy person.

How to get control of *kama* and *krodha*? Team members without thinking about external things, have to concentrate on the centre of the body and do *anulom* and *vilom* with nose. This brings mind, body and indriyas under control. Team members who are able to do this are away from *kama* and *krodha*. An individual having equality over all weather seasons, happy or unhappy, praise or insult and has stable mind can gain project knowledge well. *Yogi* has internal knowledge and wisdom. He keeps all the indriyas under control and has equality among stone, mud and gold. A *best individual* is one who has equality among friends, enemies, competitors, pleasers, mediators, relatives, sinners, followers, leaders and devotees. In our project management, a team member should exercise equality among customers, suppliers, vendors, project managers, program managers, functional heads, senior management, top management and family members.

Team members who behave wisely while eating and executing tasks can get away with unhappiness in life. Ultimate happiness is the feeling away from senses of *pancha indriyas.* This comes with only *micro vision.* An individual who looks at all the living things equally, and treats happiness or sadness equally, is a *yogi* and the *ultimate purist*. Here, the quality of "look at others happy as his happy" is the characteristic of high performance teams. This is required to achieve high performance in project teams. One cannot understand the meaning of *equality* with an unstable mind. Hence, controlling it is very difficult for anybody. To control the mind one has to have practice (*abhyasa*) and detachment (*vairagya*). *Vairagya* does not mean that leave all social and family responsibilities. It means to have detachment over affection and hate and concentrate on the task in hand. Team members having control of mind can become *yogis* with practice.

11

Critical Success Factors for Offshore Software Development Projects

Offshore project success is very much important to both customer and the vendor. Based on very less success rate of overall software projects globally, critical success factors (CSFs) for offshore software projects is gaining much importance.

11.1 Introduction

The success rate of software projects is relatively less compared with other industry projects. Because of the low percentage of success rate in software projects, project success became a topic of research for many researchers across the world. There are many factors such as technical factors, cultural factors, environmental factors, and legal and social factors affecting the success of offshore software projects in countries such as India, China, Ireland, Philippines, Taiwan, Singapore, Hong Kong, Malaysia, Israel, Brazil, Russia, Mexico, South Africa, Hungary and the Czech Republic.

The business of software development is becoming global in nature. For example, Boeing 787 Dreamliner project brings together 50 global partners working in over 130 locations across the globe. Globalization and opening up of different global markets and the global dispersed nature of software work is increasing the offshore software market.

IT organizations are using global human resources to reduce costs and improve quality. Usually, an offshore provider can be a wholly owned subsidiary, partially owned subsidiary or an entirely external service provider. Off shoring happens from a physically dispersed geographical location, different time zone and different culture. IT offshore business is led by India, followed by China and other near shore countries such as the Eastern European countries. Indian offshore industry has maintained double digit growth rate for almost two decades. Russian offshore industry is also growing with strong technical skills, methodologies, and high education levels in mathematics and science backgrounds.

With advancements in telecommunications infrastructure across the world, organizations are following the sun in their offshore software services delivery. Organizations such as IBM, HP, Accenture, CapGemini, SAP, and Oracle have off-shored their work to many service providers in Asia. The off-shoring trend has increased since the Y2K and Euro currency transition.

11.2 Features of Offshore Projects

Off-shoring phenomenon has mixed response in the world. Offshore development is labour-intensive, complex, technology-intensive, knowledge-intensive, multi-disciplinary and requires a lot of information flow. Risks are not removed totally when organizations go for off-shoring. There exists little empirical evidence in the literature which shows cost reductions with off-shoring. In fact, new set of risks get added because of cultural, language and time zone issues requiring rigorous risk management for offshore software projects. The complexity of project work increases because the teams are geographically distributed in different parts of the world.

Sometimes, off-shoring may lead to layoffs at client location, or transfer of some of the employees to vendor organization and resultantly becoming contractors for the client organization. Overall, it leads to a lot of restructuring and change of roles and responsibilities at client location and sometimes brings in a lot of confusion and ambiguity in role and responsibilities because of introduction of vendor employees in the project. Other concerns of off-shoring include data thefts, cyber crimes, intellectual property issues, network security issues and political climate.

The IT off-shoring resulting in resizing of the client staff, may lead to low morale, stress, reduced commitment, loss of trust, anxiety and resentment in retained employees at client location. Off-shoring software work brings in additional costs such as lock-in, knowledge transfer costs, technology transfer costs, transition costs, legal and liability costs, vendor management costs and cultural adaptation.

Also, customer organizations maintain a pool of offshore service providers to reduce costs, and bring in competition among service providers for enhanced performance and high quality levels. The challenges of off-shoring software projects include cultural factors, infrastructure and security issues, geographical distances, morale and public opinion. Overall, offshore software development reduces the costs of software application development.

11.3 Why Offshore Projects are Tricky?

The *offshore project success* is very tricky because the processes, resources, roles and responsibilities are divided between customer and the service provider. Project success is measured in terms of triple factors of the project such as time, cost and quality. Offshore project success can be measured in terms of cost/benefit, customer satisfaction, meeting expectations and fulfilment of psychological obligations. Offshore project success is also measured in terms of schedules, functionality, budget and quality. Project success is a combination of *product success* and *project management success*. Project success is the ability to satisfy the needs of the users. Selection of a suitable project, project definition and early decision-making are crucial to project success.

Offshore project success depends on the quality of relationship between client and vendor. High level of offshore expertise, trust between vendor and offshore service provider and knowledge transfer, are positively related to offshore software project success. Project characteristics such as project size, duration, programming language, degree of coding and suitability of project for off-shoring has a positive impact on offshore project success.

Lack of sufficient language skills leads to misunderstandings, reduced productivity, reduced quality, and increases the risks of offshore projects. The key success factor for any offshore provider is having a list of referenced customers. Research studies about cross-cultural impacts on information systems projects are very limited. Cultural diversity is good for *innovation* and *creativity* which is very much required in knowledge-based work such as software development. Client participation and involvement are very much needed for the success of offshore software projects. Trust between client and service provider influences the knowledge transfer which in turn impacts the offshore project success.

11.4 Success Factors for Offshore Software Projects

The success factors for software exports include national vision and strategy, international linkages and trust, project management, English language skills, and factors such as people, technology, research and development and finance. Many scholars have identified the need for linkage between project success criteria and critical success factors. They have given a project excellence model with critical success factors such as policy and strategy, stakeholder management, leadership and team, contracting, resources, and project management factors such as schedule, organization, quality, budget, risks and project information.

The critical success factors for offshore software projects are listed in Table 11.1.

To succeed in the global offshore market, offshore providers have to develop practices and models which are rare, valuable and difficult to copy. It is the best practice to have *exit strategies* as well while off-shoring projects and products. Critical success factors require continuous monitoring by senior management and they have to be effectively managed for offshore project success. Basically, CSFs for projects vary from industry to industry and country to country. Hence, similar research can be customized for different industries in different countries.

Table 11.1: Critical Success Factors for

Offshore Software Projects

Serial Number	Critical success factor category	Critical success factor
1.	Cultural factors	Cultural understanding. Management of cultural differences.
2.	Language factors	Overcome language barriers. Language skills.
3.	Time zone factors	Managing different time zones. Time zone multiplicities.
4.	Organizational factors	Trust building. Relationship between client and vendor.
5.	Environmental factors	Legal environment. Telecom infrastructure.
6.	Communication factors	Efficient communication. Communication technologies.
7.	Technology transfer factors	Technical skills. Data privacy and security.
8.	Knowledge transfer factors	Efficient knowledge transfer. Domain knowledge.
9.	Project factors	Project planning/management. Risk sharing/management.
10.	Team factors	Team competencies. Management change.

11.5 Success Story of India as Provider of Software Services

India has emerged in recent years as the most preferred destination for outsourcing of IT services. The vibrant IT industry is contributing immensely by providing information about latest technology and international business practices.

Starting out with basic data entry tasks, the IT industry has rapidly acquired a reputation as the primary low-cost destination for voice-based customer contact/support services, finance and accounting, and a range of back-office processing activities. The past few years have seen the scope of these services expanding to include increasingly more complex processes involving rule-based decision-making and research/analytics services requiring informed individual judgment and domain/vertical knowledge. Key categories within horizontal IT services include: (a) customer interaction and support (CIS), (b) finance and accounting (F&A) and other related processing services, (c) knowledge services and (d) human resource management (HRM).

With experience and maturity, several providers are also beginning to develop increasing vertical specialization, thereby complementing their horizontal IT service offerings with vertical specific services.

Much of the IT work is of a routine nature such as customer contact services, but increasingly the outsourced jobs are getting sophisticated. The main knowledge services already outsourced to Indian companies are animation and simulation services, data research and analytics, and litigation services. Other possibilities are in intellectual property research, medical content and services, pharmaceutical services, writing/content development services, database development services and end-to-end logistic invoice services. A major impediment in India making progress from data processing and customer contact services to knowledge process services is the deficiency in qualified talent in both quantitative and qualitative terms in economics and statistics, law, medical science, pharmacy, media and English language in particular.

11.6 Strategies of Indian IT Companies

Indian companies adopt all the modes for supply of IT services abroad. The larger companies have set up wholly-owned subsidiaries in US, UK and European continent or have opened branches to facilitate the supply of services. Some of them have adopted the strategy of acquiring local companies or entering into strategic partnerships with them. They use quality processes, innovative technologies and delivery models of acquired companies to penetrate into the local market. They have permanent employees or hire consultants based in the host country.

All four modes of supply—cross-border (Mode 1), consumption abroad (Mode 2), establishment (Mode 3) and movement of natural persons (Mode 4)—are used. In the case of IT services, Indian companies deploy human resources principally from India and sometimes from other foreign bases in order to provide on-site services and also send people for business visits, prospecting, and sales.

In US and UK, the operations are facilitated by friendlier policies on these aspects, and EU is known to be considering the introduction of the *blue card*—an EU-wide work permit. However, so far, the immigration policies in Europe have remained problematic because of long timelines, absence of internal market mobility and non-transparent and discretionary approval processes. A similar difference has existed regards the investment procedures in US and those in the countries in the European continent.

The Indian IT industry has steadily moved up the value chain and is now fully capable of envisioning and developing a whole range of value added services that can be delivered through computers, mobile phones or other devices. The industry can create and sustain a service delivery platform for such services thereby extending the global reach of the entire service industry. The advent of cloud computing technology has thrown up another wide range of possibilities for India. Indian companies have already begun creating new products and services incorporating their own IPs and patents.

12

Scientific versus Social Science Research Methodology

The multiple research methodologies used in scientific and social science research such as conceptual research, empirical research, model research methodology, experimental research, formal methodologies, build research methodology, process research methodology and simulation method are discussed in this chapter.

12.1 Introduction

Is there any clear demarcation between scientific research methodology and social science research methodology? Are they complementary or competitive?

Science is derived from different domains and uses research methods such as experimental, theoretical and simulation. Any science consists of body of knowledge. Ancient philosophers such as Aristotle, Plato, and Socrates studied domains such as astronomy, philosophy, mathematics, logic and medicine. Aristotle and Galileo were the initial contributors of scientific research. Presently, researchers are studying basic sciences, core sciences, engineering sciences, applied sciences, social sciences, natural sciences, biological sciences, zoological sciences, medical and health sciences. Modern social sciences include history, political science, sociology, anthropology, psychology, linguistics, philosophy and cultural studies.

Information systems research requires combination of technological and social issues. It is derived from the domains such as cognitive science, computer science, ergonomics, organizational theory, management science, political science, economics, organization science, psychology, language theory and organizational behaviour. Information systems research can also be technical or behavioural in nature. The research process involves revising theories, facts and applications. The goal of current day research is discovery and dissemination of knowledge and information. The traditional research concentrated on finding and developing knowledge on the unknowns.

12.2 Conceptual Research

It is useful for making derivations, definitions, propositions and deriving hypotheses based on literature gaps. This basically identifies the basic constructs in the subject knowledge base and finds the interconnections and links between constructs, factors and variables. Conceptual research is useful to make conceptual models pertaining to the subject area. Further, conceptual models are used to do empirical, causal and experimental research. Conceptual research is the primary step for empirical, causal or experimental research.

Based on the results of the experiments and observation, the hypotheses are adjusted in scientific research. Adjusting the hypotheses is not possible in management research after data analysis. In management or social sciences research, the hypotheses are either supported or not supported after data analysis. The hypothesis is consistent here.

Scientific theory is based on empirical knowledge coming out of observational experimentation. The scientific research cycle is recursive in nature. The research methods followed in scientific research are mostly quantitative in nature. Research methods followed in social sciences are mostly qualitative in nature. There are cases where mixed methods are also followed in both scientific and social sciences research.

12.3 Empirical Research

Empirical research is mostly used in social sciences, behavioural sciences, sociology, psychology, industrial psychology and economics. It is based on data collection, hypothesis proving based on data and deriving conclusions from it. For example, for the past two decades, extensive empirical research is going on in areas such as software engineering, computer science and information systems. This indicates that engineering and scientific research is also using empirical methods. Empirical research methods are used in project management research also. Experimental software engineering brings in domains such as sociology, economics, psychology, and computer science.

Empirical research uses techniques such as questionnaires, interviews and case studies. Using questionnaires, nominal, continuous, ordinal, interval, ratio and discrete data are collected. This data is further analysed for hypotheses testing and deriving conclusions using statistical techniques. Empirical research considering organizational and societal variables should be able to analyze the qualitative comments and textual inputs.

12.4 Model Research Methodology

Model research methodology is used to define an abstract view of a complex system. Models are built to avoid higher costs in building the entire complex system. These models can be used to test and modify and further used for simulation purposes. Models are also required for experimentation. Model research methodology is normally used in combination with other research methodologies such as experimental, empirical, etc. The models built in scientific research or engineering research are physical models different from the conceptual models developed in management or social science research.

In management or social science research, conceptual models can be represented as written text or diagrams. Whereas, in scientific research, models are represented in the form of physical things. In case of computer science, models can be software applications running with minimal functionality. Model is built as an interacting component. It can also be a data model. Using models, one can test the what-if scenarios, do experimentation and also engage in simulations. Model is an abstraction of a real world thing. Model is an instrument used or developed by the researchers. It is not the final objective of a research. Models often give qualitative and quantitative details to the researchers.

Either in management research or in scientific research, modelling a research problem should be the first step. After modelling, further research methods/methodologies can be applied to either conceptual model or a physical scientific model.

12.5 Experimental Research

Experimental research methodology is a common research methodology followed in both sciences and social sciences. However, in most of the cases, it is applicable to scientific research. Experimental research has two phases in it. They are exploratory phase and evaluation phase. In *exploratory phase*, the researcher thinks about the questions to ask about the system to be evaluated and in *evaluation phase* he finds the answers to those questions.

To make ground breaking innovations like the ones did by Thomas Alva Edison and Albert Einstein, research has to be purely laboratory-based, changing the experimental conditions all the time. This kind of experimentation requires a lot of patience and dedication. Unless these are present, future generations may not see ground breaking innovations which make life better. When the survival is the biggest question, very few individuals are dedicating and venturing into these kinds of research methodologies.

Maintaining records of experimental results is very much important in execution of the experiment. This record keeping should be in such a way so that the experimental results can be retrieved at a later date. Repeating the experiments in social sciences or management research is not possible or difficult because of the changing organizational conditions. However, in scientific research, the experiments can be repeated under the same conditions. The steps in experimentation include experiment definition, experiment planning, experiment operation, result analysis, result interpretation, and outcome recording.

12.6 Formal Methodologies

Formal methodologies are used in computer science to verify certain facts before automatic verification such as finding the algorithm time and space complexity. Formal methodologies are widely used in theoretical computer science. Formal methodologies also make use of building abstract and mathematical models. These formal methodologies are used to find efficient algorithms in areas such as distributed systems, parallel computing, cryptography, combinatorial and geometry.

12.7 Build Research Methodology

In scientific research, build research methodology is also followed to build a new artefact which is not present earlier. The artefact built using this approach should have unique features which none of the artefacts have them earlier. In computer science research, build research is widely used to design and build software systems. While building the software systems, the software components can be reused, specific programming language is selected and continuous testing is done to the software system.

12.8 Process Research Methodology

Process research methodology is used in certain areas such as artificial intelligence, software quality, software process improvement and software engineering to find out the processes accomplishing things. Process research methodology is widely used where human interaction is more. It is used in human-computer interaction, vision, and cognitive sciences.

12.9 Simulation Methodology

Simulation methodology is used wherein real implementation is complex, time consuming and costly. For example, in domains such as astronomy, economics, and physics, computer simulation methods are widely used.

There are other research methodologies such as action research, interpretative research, grounded theory, protocol analysis and ethnography used in scientific research. The main skills required for researchers in both scientific and social science research are the expressive, cognitive, organizational and meta-cognitive skills. The specific skills required for researchers in these areas include scanning papers, searching papers, critique literature, design models, data collection, data analysis, drawing conclusions, interpreting results, finding literature gaps, linking to previous research and building body of knowledge. The researchers filter the world through their conceptual lens.

Thus, empirical and experiment research methodologies are used in both scientific and social science research. Simulation is used in both economics and computer science. These findings indicate that there is no clear demarcation or the demarcation is very less in the methodologies used in scientific and social science research. All the methodologies are helping the researchers in both the areas in using, interpreting and making right conclusions.

13

Research in Management: From Identification to Publication

How to do research in management? Why to do research in management? What research is to be done? What is the need for doing research in management? What comes out of management research? Is it useful or applicable? What skills are required for an individual to do research in management? These are some of the questions faced in day to day life by research scholars, working professionals, functional managers such as marketing managers, HR managers, finance managers, operations managers, project managers, and executives in the industry. This chapter tries to answers all these questions.

13.1 Problem Definition

Management research can be *exploratory* or *conclusive*. That means we do research either to find a problem in the system/environment/industry or to find a solution for a specific problem. *Exploratory research* deals with finding different problems currently present or obstructing an organization. In what areas/sectors the organization can expand? This leads to exploratory research. Why sales are down in specific regions? This type of problem leads to *conclusive research* resulting in solutions to the problem at the end of the research process. A management researcher has to decide first whether he is finding a problem or finding a solution to the existing problem.

Research can also be *empirical* (primary) or *literature review* (secondary) based. Empirical or primary research is done through data collection, data analysis and finding results. Whereas secondary research is done through secondary sources of data such as previous literature, papers, articles, databases, magazines and newspapers. In secondary research, no data is directly collected from the sample or population. In primary research, data is collected directly from the sample of population. Primary research can also be *quantitative research* because of the statistical techniques used in data collection. Similarly, secondary research can be *qualitative research* as well. No statistical techniques may be used but inferences or conclusions can be made.

What is the need for doing research in management? The need is to find the existing problem because of which organizational profitability, earnings, reputation or business is getting impacted or to find the solution to identified problem using statistical techniques. In case of Ph.D. in management, one has to identify the research problem first. To do this, one has to first identify the industry or domain such as IT, healthcare, finance, telecom, retail, utilities, banking, manufacturing etc. in which he or she would like to do research. After choosing the industry, one has to select a business function such as HR, finance, marketing, operations, IT etc. in which he or she would like to do the research.

This kind of narrowing down of areas is the best practice in identifying or finding the research problem. For example, one can select a topic in HR aspects in the banking industry. Or one can select a topic in marketing factors in telecom or mobile phone industry. Alternatively, one can select a topic in patience satisfaction in healthcare industry. Thus, one has to narrow down the industry and business function in which he or she would like to do the research.

After finding the industry and business function, the research scholar has to do thorough literature review of his or her own interest areas in the narrowed down domain. Selection of specific topic and research problem description are very important in Ph.D. or research journey. If the problem description is itself ambiguous the researcher may not get the needed output out of the research process. For selecting a specific topic, the researcher has to use some keywords in the area and search for scholarly articles in that domain using internet search engines such as Google, Yahoo, Microsoft Academic Search, and Google Scholar. These days many scholarly journals and papers are available for download over the internet. Some of the journals may be paid; however, sufficient papers are available free of cost over the internet.

13.2 Literature Review

Though literature review is required for describing the research problem, after glancing 30 to 40 papers in the specific area, one can find the literature gaps using scope for further research given in the collected literature. Usually, sections such as scope for further research, research limitations, and future directions given in the papers generate new ideas and thoughts in the mind of a researcher.

Hence, these sections are not to be overlooked or ignored in the papers. Thus, one can define the research problem by identifying the gaps in the literature. Having around 200 references for a Ph.D. thesis is good. The collected articles/papers should be from authentic source and they should be scholarly. Usually, the reviewers also judge your paper or thesis based on the quality of referred papers.

13.3 Conceptual Model Development

This is the first step in management research. Any research work should have a conceptual research model. From the problem description point of view, the researcher has to identify the components, factors and dimensions which constitute a research problem. The model pictorially represents the relationships, associations and containments between the components and factors in the research problem. For example, *organizational environment* constitutes economic, political, social, and cultural environment.

Similarly *organizational culture* includes values and belief systems of the employees. Thus, one has to identify the components, dimensions and factors in the research problem and has to draw the associations in the block diagram. This makes the conceptual model for a research problem. Some even have complex mathematical or economic models as well. In the conceptual model, some components may be dependent variables and some may be independent variables. Next step would be defining the hypotheses.

13.4 Define Hypotheses

Hypothesis is the statement which the researcher is going to prove or disprove. Defining hypotheses from the problem description is an important step in research process. Usually, having 8 to 10 major hypotheses are good for a Ph.D. research work. Sometimes, major hypotheses can be further decomposed into sub-hypotheses. Mainly the hypotheses are derived based on the relationships or associations between different components and factors in the conceptual model.

For example, a hypothesis may be finding the relationship between employee engagement and job satisfaction. Or other hypothesis may be finding the impact of employee involvement on project performance. Another hypothesis can be impact of HR policies on employee turnover. Thus, one has to define the hypotheses for the given problem. It is the best practice to number hypotheses as Hypothesis 1, Hypothesis 2, Hypothesis 3, etc.

13.5 Research Design and Methodology

Once the hypotheses are derived, research methodology, design or approach has to be defined. A research design consists of sample determination, data collection procedure, data analysis procedure and statistical techniques to be used for data analysis. The sample to collect the data is to be identified from the specific geography or specific associations or bodies or organizations. Once the sample determination is done, the data collection procedure is to be defined.

There are different ways to collect data from sample of population. Some of them are structured questionnaires, interviews and case study or experimental approaches. Before data collection, the questionnaire has to be designed and tested as a pilot run by collecting data from 30 to 40 individuals or organizations whatever the case may be. The number of questions, the types of questions and answer scale, that is, 5-point Likert scale or 7-point scale has to be decided while designing the questionnaire.

Once questionnaire design is done, it has to be administered as a pilot run and checked for the reliability, validity and consistency of the instrument. The questionnaire is also called an instrument here. The questionnaire can also be taken or derived from previous literature with proper permissions. The reliability of the instrument is checked using Cronbach Alpha. If the Cronbach Alpha is near to 0.9, the instrument is reliable. The validity is of two types. They are *convergent validity* and *divergent validity*. Convergent validity checks the relationships (correlation) between the factors within the components and the divergent validity checks the relationship (correlation) between the different components in the model.

The convergent validity should have maximum values and divergent validity should have minimum values. After checking the instrument's reliability and validity, the researcher can administer the questionnaire for the entire sample.

13.6 Data Collection, Correction and Preparation

Presently, data collection using online surveys reduces the error rate in data entry. For example, websites such as www.kiwksurveys.com and www.surveymonkey.com provide facilities for having online questionnaires and collect the data over internet from anywhere in the world. The collected data can be exported to excel sheets from these websites. Once data is in excel sheet form, it can further be imported into SPSS or any other analysis tools such as LISREL and AMOS (Structured Equation Modelling Tools).

The data in the excel sheet can be verified and corrected for completion purpose. The incomplete entries if any can be removed from the data sheet and the data is further prepared for analysis purpose. This is very much important for getting correct and accurate results. This also avoids future data processing errors from the statistical packages.

13.7 Data Analysis by Statistical Techniques

Usually, the prepared data is analysed using statistical packages such as IBM SPSS. Here, statistical techniques such as mean, median, mode, standard deviation, variance, correlation, regression, ANOVA (Analysis of Variance), t-test, Chi Square test, multivariate analysis, and multiple regressions, can be used. For example, correlation is used to find the relationship between two different variables or components. If the correlation coefficient value is more than 0.75, the relationship is treated as a strong relationship. If the correlation coefficient is in between 0.5 and 0.75 the relationship is treated as a moderate relationship and if the correlation coefficient is less than 0.5 the relationship is a weak relationship between the variables.

Similarly, regression is used to find the impact of one variable on another variable. If the significant value (p-value) is less than 0.05, it indicates that there exists an impact of the variable on the other variable. Similar conclusions can be drawn from the statistical values. These statistical techniques are used for hypotheses proving.

13.8 Confirmatory Factor Analysis

Confirmatory factor analysis (CFA) is done to check the factor loadings after data collection. This checks whether the data fits the measurement model or not. CFA can be done using LISREL software package. LISREL can also be used for structured equation modelling (SEM). SEM models give path diagrams and path coefficients.

They show the intensity of relationships between different components and variables. LISREL tests whether the data fits the structured equation model or not. Using SEM, one can generate path diagrams and it can also be used for hypothesis proving. Usually, CFA is done before data analysis to check the fitment of the model or to drop some variables from the model/data.

13.9 Research Findings

Using statistical techniques and SEM, one can prove the hypotheses. From hypotheses proving and also from generated statistical tables, further conclusions and findings can be drawn. For example, correlation tables depict the relationships between different factors in the model. From this also, some interesting conclusions can be drawn. The research findings can be summarized and documented. These should be included in the thesis or paper to be published.

13.10 Publishing Research Papers

To gain an early entrant advantage, the researcher has to publish the research results as soon as they are out. This can be done by publishing in national or international journals. Very few researchers from India are trying to publish in high impact factor journals such as *Academy of Management Journal, Academy of Management Review, Harvard Business Review, MIS Quarterly, International Journal of Project Management, etc.* There are also high impact international journals from Emerald, Elsevier, Springer, Taylor and Francis, SAGE, Macmillan-Palgrave and IGI Global.

Some of the researchers from India are publishing their work with these publishers. Sometimes publishing in open access journals can give more citations to a researcher's work. Some researchers are also publishing in national and international conferences and seminars. Some researchers in India are publishing their management research work in AIMA journals and *Indian Management*.

In the thesis or in published papers, the researcher has to mention the implications for industry, implications for research community, implications for academia, limitations of the current research and scope for further research. It is a good practice to have 5 to 6 papers published for approval of Ph.D. thesis. These publications support the thesis and make an evaluators' job easy.

Part III
People Aspects in Project Management

14

People Side of Modern Project Management

This chapter is about people-related aspects of project management. Every project starts with recruiting people for a project. Consequently, the selection, induction, setting of objectives, work allocation and performance appraisals etc. takes place. People in the project communicate with each other. The communication path can be horizontal or vertical (upward or downward).

There are millions of dollars spent on different projects every year across the globe. All these projects are being executed by the men and the machines. There is hardly any project being executed without human resources involved in it. Hence, people are most important in a project environment. A project becomes a success or a failure because of the people issues. Hence, people side of project management has significant importance in project management area.

14.1 Recruitment

Recruitment is the first step in people aspect of project management. The project starts by taking people into the system. First, the project management team advertises about the vacancies in the project to the external world. Whether it is internal recruitment or external recruitment, the management team notifies the vacancies to the outer world. The probable candidates then apply for the vacancies. The project management team selects the suitable candidates from the available candidate pool.

Usually, selection into the project may come through the organizational human resource (HR) process or by direct selection tests of the project. There are different types of selection tests. They are aptitude tests and personality tests. Aptitude test tests a candidate's numerical, logical, critical reasoning and analytical skills. Personality tests include psychometric tests. Generally, in IT organizations, for programmer positions, different projects follow different tests. Some may conduct written tests in specific programming language and others may conduct interviews for selection purposes.

14.2 Induction

Once the candidate is selected, he comes on board the organization and subsequently into the project. First, the HR department of an organization gives the organization level induction to the candidates. Once this is over, the candidate joins the specific project formally.

Subsequently, the project manager provides him the induction training into the project. This induction specifically communicates the common terminology the project uses or any ground rules already in place in the project for the newly joined team member.

This way, the newly joined team member comes to know about the project, people in the project and little bit about the processes involved in the project and the organization. Usually, induction happens after the introduction of new team members is over with the other existing team members. Senior members of the project, the project management team, team leaders, technical leaders or architects are involved in giving the induction to the new team members.

Once the formal induction is over, the newly joined team member will be in a position to learn the project documentation and he is aware of the sources of information in the project. After few weeks, he starts working on the given tasks for him under the guidance of the manager and the architect. Here, the project manager plays a key role in making the new team member feel comfortable in the project. This is very much required for the team member to become absorbed in the project or the organization.

14.3 Setting Objectives

Once the induction is over, it is better to set the formal goals and objectives for the new team member. Usually, the project manager sets the objectives for the team member for the coming appraisal period or for the coming one-year time. These objectives are documented and filed with the HR department of the organization. This process is very much needed because a team member's performance needs to be evaluated at the time of performance appraisals against these objectives set earlier. Hence, objectives setting process is very much important for an individual team member's development.

14.4 Work Allocation

Once goal setting is over, the individual comes to know what is expected out of him in the coming six months to one-year time. Then the project manager assigns the tasks from the work break down structure to the team members. That is, the project manager delegates the work to the team members based on the project plan. Delegation of work needs a lot of courage from the project manager's side.

While accepting the work, the individual team members exhibit different behaviour in different situations. One accepts the work, without even thinking about the outcome of the work. Another member may simply reject to the assigned work. Some members may negotiate and then accept the given task. Yet another member may delay the acceptance of the assigned task. Thus, different team members exhibit different behaviour in different circumstances based on the nature of the task, and environmental circumstances.

Because of this, the project manager should take into consideration the interests of the team members and their past experiences while assigning tasks to them. Once tasks are delegated, the team members start executing the assigned tasks and update the progress to the project manager.

While executing the tasks, different team members exhibit

different behaviour. This behaviour is based on the level of knowledge of the team member for a given task, his confidence level, time constraints, customer pressure, peer pressure and his relationship with the project manager. All these factors can affect an individual's behaviour while executing the given project tasks.

Usually, the confident team members deliver the results without even informing the hurdles they encountered while executing the tasks. Reaching this level is completely based on the knowledge of the individual, his practice over specific technology and understanding of the systems and subsystems interconnections, etc.

14.5 Communicating with Other Team Members

Team members come under two categories. Either they are introvert or extravert. Introverts in technical teams remain with the books and manuals. When they encounter technical problems, they try to explore on their own with the help of manuals.

Extraverts immediately discuss the technical problem they are encountering in the project with other team members and then try to find the solution for the problem. Sometimes introverts may stress on perfection in dealing with technical issues. This kind of behaviour is observed in technical teams in the projects.

Similarly, team members communicate with each other formally or informally. This communication flows horizontally and vertically in the project. In horizontal communication, team members communicate with their peers over technical matters. The vertical communication may flow over in an upward or downward direction. The technical leaders communicate with their managers and subordinates in the project environment.

Overall, the project manager has to excel in human relations. Since, he will be talking to the team members regularly he should have good communication and leadership skills.

14.6 Facing Conflicts

In team environment, there is possibility for conflicts among team members in the project. Some of the conflicts may have positive outcomes in the sense of more productive ideas. Some of the conflicts may have negative impact on the project and its team members. It all depends on the way conflicts are handled. Hence, a project manager should have the conflict resolution skills.

A *conflicting* situation is one in which two or more parties look for the outcome to come in their favour. Then the manager has to facilitate and try to resolve the conflicting situation. There can be many reasons for conflicts. The resources, schedules, project issues, technical issues, administrative procedures, project costs, performance appraisals and personality issues etc. can be some of the reasons for conflicts. If a team member is not happy with his peer then he exhibits anger over his supervisor. If the team member is not happy with any of the company policies or procedures, then he exhibits different behaviour with his immediate supervisor.

14.7 Conflict Resolution Techniques

Once conflict occurs, the manager can use conflict resolution techniques which include the following:

1. Confrontation,
2. Compromise,
3. Smoothing,
4. Forcing, or
5. Withdrawal.

By using the *confrontation* technique, one keeps the facts and figures in picture and resolves the conflict. This technique creates a win-win situation for the parties in the conflicting situation.

In *compromise* technique, both the parties go a step backward and settle the situation.

In *smoothing* technique, the parties in conflict discuss the situation and go back to their cubicles thinking that the conflict is resolved. After spending some time, they think that the conflict still exists and it was not resolved earlier. This technique may not be recommended all the times.

By using the *forcing* technique, the manager can force his team members and win the argument. This creates a win-loose situation. This may not be applied all the times.

Another conflict resolution technique is *withdrawal.* Using this technique, one just withdraws from the argument and the other party wins the argument. This creates a loose-win situation.

Using these conflict resolution techniques, one can come out of the conflicts and make the conflicts useful for productivity improvement purposes.

14.8 Performance Appraisals

Once a team member spends considerable amount of time in a project, it is time to evaluate his performance against the objectives set earlier. This is the job of his manager, peers and subordinates. Usually, different companies follow different performance appraisal methods to evaluate team members' performance.

Self-appraisal, supervisor's appraisal and reviewer's comments will be there in this process. In majority of IT organizations, for team members' performance appraisal, the manager is given the feedback. For middle-level managers, a 360-degree feedback is taken. It varies from organization to organization.

The main objective of these performance appraisals is to find out the training needs of individual team members and to check whether they are meeting the project and organizational objectives or not. We can observe many conflicting situations in the case of performance appraisal discussions in an organization. Promotions, demotions, salary hikes and transfers in the organization are based on performance appraisals.

14.9 Motivating Team Members

Motivating knowledge workers, such as IT engineers, is a challenging task for a project manager. In most cases, the knowledge worker is self-managed. However, the manager has to motivate and encourage his team members also. Some of the motivating activities the managers in IT industry can do are mentioned below.

1. Sending programmers to seminars or conferences to apprise them of the latest technology.
2. Giving work in their interested areas instead of legacy systems.
3. Giving project bonus and frenzy benefits.
4. Giving on-site assignments and sending them abroad.
5. Giving cross-functional assignments.
6. Moving across teams.
7. Moving across different technologies.
8. Moving across different customer accounts.

14.10 Training and Development

Based on the performance appraisals, we can identify the training needs of the specific team members. Once we have done the appraisals for all team members, the project manager can update the training plan for the team member. The HR department comes up with training calendars once they receive all appraisals forms from the respective project managers. The team members can be provided training in latest technologies depending on project needs. Some of the IT companies make certain days of training mandatory for the software engineers in their organizations. This is required for the development of an individual and also for new upcoming projects of the organization.

14.11 Moving Between Projects

Once a team member spends sufficient time in one project, it is better for him to move to the other project in the organization. This change is good for the long-term benefit of a team member. Similarly, it is a good practice to move the project managers across different customer accounts. With this, managers learn diversified skills and cultures.

It is better to move a team member to another project, if he is not confident of the technologies in which he/she is currently working and if he/she is under performing. Sometimes, if an organization gets a key project from a new customer, then also they pick key team members from different projects and form a new team for the new customer. Accordingly, a project manager has to use his negotiation skills in retaining and acquiring key team members.

15

Different Dimensions of Teams

Popularity of team work is growing in the 21st century. Organizations are getting their work done through different types of teams. Teams have proved that collective performance is more than the sum of individual performances. Thus, the teams have got different dimensions such as quantitative dimensions and qualitative dimensions. The quantitative dimensions of teams include team performance, team productivity, team innovation, team effectiveness, team efficiency, team decision-making and team conflicts. Qualitative dimensions of teams include team communication, team coordination, team cooperation, team cohesion, team climate, team creativity, team leadership and team conflicts.

15.1 Meaning and Characteristics of a Team

A team is a collection of individuals working towards a common purpose and goal. Different types of teams include work groups, project teams, parallel teams, management teams and ad-hoc teams. One can find work groups in manufacturing industry, project teams in construction and software industries, parallel teams in research, management teams in top management of an organization and ad-hoc teams in public sector and governments across the world.

The characteristics of teams include the following:

1. Team has a common purpose.
2. Team has a common goal to achieve.
3. Team consists of human resources.
4. Team is lead by a team leader or team manager.
5. Team objectives are in line with organizational objectives.
6. Team strategies are in line with organizational strategies.
7. Team requires resources such as time, money, material,

hardware, software, tools, machinery etc.

A team in any industry takes human resources, raw material, time, money, hardware, software, machinery, and tools as inputs. It processes the input resources using skills, knowledge, experience, competencies, and techniques and produces the desired outputs. The outputs of teamwork can be products, services, results, technical procedures, business processes, methodologies, procedures, platforms or any frameworks useful to the stakeholders, customers, or internal users.

Organizations are always looking at the performance and productivity of teams for better organizational outcomes, results and customer satisfaction.

As already noted, different dimensions of a team can be categorized into quantitative dimensions and qualitative dimensions.

15.2 Quantitative Dimensions of a Team

15.2.1 Team Performance: Team performance is different at different stages of team development. At the forming stage of team development, team performance is the minimum and after crossing the storming stages of team development, team enters into the peak level of performance. Usually, there are different measures for team performance. These measures can be categorized as objective measures and subjective measures.

Objective measures of team performance include measures of productivity, return on investment, response time, turnaround time, profits made by the team, earnings from the team, cost reductions by the team, increase in market capitalization by the team, increase in share value, number of new processes developed, and number of tools developed.

Subjective measures of team performance include the feedback or ratings given by different stakeholders such as team members, customers, senior management, suppliers, project managers, and other stakeholders, if any. Customer satisfaction index or customer satisfaction ratings are subjective measures of team performance. It is good to have both subjective and objective measures while measuring team performance in an organization.

15.2.2 Team Productivity: Team productivity is the quotient of the output divided by the input.

Team productivity = Output/Input

That is, team productivity is the number of units produced per unit time of input or per unit input resource. For example, the productivity of software teams is measured in terms of KLOC (kilo lines of code) per man hour in old days, and in current days productivity of software teams is measures in terms of FPs (function points) implemented in a man day. Similarly, construction team productivity can be measured in terms of cubic foot constructed per man hour or man day. Every industry has got similar measures to determine team productivity. For example, in manufacturing industry, team productivity can be measured in terms of number of units produced per man hour.

15.2.3 Team Innovation: Innovation is the number of creative ideas implemented. Creativity is the generation of ideas and thoughts in new ways of doing things. Innovation is implementation of the generated ideas to develop a product, service, process, intermediate product or work deliverable. Team innovation can be measured in terms of number of patents filed, number of patents approved, number of international papers published, number of national papers published, number of research reports generated, impact of the research, sales growth, market growth, new markets entered, power saving, cost savings, resources saving, procedures reduced, etc. For example, research team innovation can be measured in terms of number of publications, number of patents received, impact of research, number of products developed based on research, time taken to develop a product, time to enter the market, and sales growth.

Usually, innovative teams perform better because team innovation is positively correlated to team performance.

Similarly, team productivity is positively associated with team performance.

15.2.4 Team Effectiveness: Effectiveness can be measured in terms of performance, productivity and customer satisfaction. For example, a senior manager may ask "Has the training given to team proved effective?" This would determine the percentage growth in terms of performance and productivity of the team after training was given. To measure the effectiveness, one has to take the samples at different intervals of time and has to make note of the inputs or training given to the team. Team performance or productivity has to be measured before the change and after the change and the difference notifies whether the team was effective or not. If the difference depicts a positive growth, then we can conclude that the team was effective. If the difference shows a negative growth, then the team was ineffective.

15.2.5 Team Efficiency: For the input resources given, is there any improvement in productivity or performance. Or for example, what is the performance of an engine per litre of fuel. Thus, team efficiency can be measured by per unit of money spent or unit of time spent on team. Team efficiency is also a quantitative measure of team. At one point of time team may be efficient and at another point of time the team may be inefficient. It is basically the reaction from team for the input given.

15.2.6 Team Decision-Making: Team decision-making is basically a collective effort from the team. Team decisions can impact individuals, teams, organizations, customers, suppliers or any other stakeholders. Decision-making can be quantified in team using decision trees. Decision can be financial or non-financial. Participative safety is very much required for a team to take unbiased decisions. Team vision has also got impact on team decision-making. It is basically a team process which can result into monetary or non-monetary activities or tasks. Decisions can lead to change management in the team or in the overall organization. Team decision-making is required to achieve high performance in teams. A manager only taking decisions may not make the team a high performing team.

15.2.7 Team Conflicts: Conflict is a state of disagreement with other party because of several reasons. The reasons for conflicts in teams can be shared or common resources, schedules, costs, technical opinions, administrative issues, personality issues, technical procedures, management decisions, cultural issues, and task sharing. Team communication can lead to conflicts in teams. Conflicts are of the following three types:

1. Task conflicts.
2. Relationship conflicts.
3. Process conflicts.

Task conflicts arise because of technical tasks or activities in picture. Educational diversity in team leads to task conflicts. Task conflict is good for team performance.

Relationship conflicts come because of demographic diversities such as age, gender, language, culture etc. Relationship conflicts reduce team performance.

Process conflicts arise due to difference of opinions in doing things. Up to a certain level of process, conflict is good for team performance. Whereas, high levels of relationship conflicts and process conflicts in teams can lead to reduced team performance. High levels of task conflicts at the initial stages of team development are good for team performance. The number of task conflicts, relationship conflicts and process conflicts in team can be quantified. For better team performance, one has to try for higher levels of task conflicts, moderate levels of process conflicts and low levels of relationship conflicts in the team. This gives optimum results and solutions for the team.

Similarly, every conflict has got depth and severity associated with it. This gives a qualitative dimension for the conflicts. More severe conflicts results into reduced team performance if they are not solved. More depth conflicts require large amounts of change management in the team and organization. Thus, a project manager has to deal with the conflicts in a careful way and use some conflict resolution techniques such as confrontation, forcing, smoothing, compromise and withdrawal. *Confrontation* only results in a win-win situation for both the parties without any side effects. In the next section, qualitative dimensions of teams are discussed.

15.3 Qualitative Dimensions of a Team

15.3.1 Team Communication: Team communication is a very important dimension for any project team. Usually, a project fails not because of technical reasons, but because of people reasons. Hence, effective communication is very important for a project success. If there are 'n' number of team members in the team, there will be n * (n-1)/2 number of communication channels in the team. Both quality and quantity of communication are important for team success. Complex project development requires continuous communication in the team. A project manager spends 90 percent of his or her time in communication. Communication in the team leads to conflicts in team. They can be task conflicts or relationship conflicts. One can measure the frequency of communication in team and its impact on team performance.

15.3.2 Team Coordination: Team coordination is very much important and required for team performance and productivity. Coordination requires vision in the team. Team coordination deals with dependencies in tasks and resources of the team. It also deals with the ownership of the tasks and activities in the picture. It also concentrates on executing dependent tasks with shared resources, availability of resources, scheduling of the activities and dealing with slags and floats. Team coordination can be measured in terms of success of the project tasks.

15.3.3 Team Cooperation: The dependencies among the project tasks include finish-start, finish-finish, start-finish, and start-start. Because of these dependencies and also based on the complexity of tasks, cooperation between team members is very much required. Lack of cooperation in teams leads to delayed projects, unfinished work products, poor quality deliverables, cost overruns, unsatisfied customer, unhealthy competition and reduced team performance. Team cooperation also determines the climate of a team. When dependent tasks are there, cooperation plays a vital role in team success. This is a qualitative dimension of a team.

15.3.4 Team Cohesion: Team cohesion determines team climate and task performance. Cohesion up to some extent is good for team performance and project success. High level of cohesion leads to resistance to change and reduced innovation in the team. Cohesion can be of two types, viz. task cohesion and social cohesion. Task cohesion is good for team performance and for completion of tasks or activities. Social cohesion in team arises because of similarities in demographic details. Task cohesion comes because of diversity in education, experience and skills. Task cohesion leads to task conflicts and social cohesion leads to relationship conflicts in the team. Task cohesion, generating task conflicts is good for team performance. And social cohesion generating relationship conflicts is not good for team performance. Usually, socially cohesive teams resist change and new ways of doing things. However, occasional informal talks between team members are required for team cooperation.

15.3.5 Team Climate: Positive team climate results in better team performance, productivity, innovation, customer satisfaction and better quality products. Team climate consists of components such as vision, task orientation, support for innovation and participative safety. Support for innovation is very much required to make a team more innovative. Participative safety is required for quality decision-making, conflict resolution and team performance. Task orientation is positively related to team productivity and vision is positively related to team performance.

Team climate can be measured using an instrument called team climate inventory (TCI). Team climate is the predictor of team performance, team productivity and customer satisfaction. If team climate is good, customer satisfaction will be good. If customer satisfaction is good, then also team climate is good. Thus, the relationship is reciprocal here.

Team climate variants include team climate for safety, team climate for participation, team climate for performance, and team climate for ethics. For selecting suitable team members for a team, team selection inventory (TSI) can be used.

15.3.6 Team Creativity: Creativity basically denotes generating new ideas and thoughts in newer ways of doing things. Team creativity is very much required for team innovation. If creativity is not there, there is no innovation. Hence, team creativity is positively associated with team innovation. Team creativity can be measured in terms of new ideas and thoughts generated. Whereas, team innovation can be measured in terms of number of patents, number of research publications, and sales growth, etc. Team creativity is positively associated with team innovation, team innovation is positively correlated to team productivity, and team productivity is in turn positively related to team performance. This is true in case of teams in many industries such as software and construction industry.

15.3.7 Team Leadership: Effective leadership is very much required for team performance. The leadership style, attitude and behaviour of leader do have an impact on team performance and project success. Visionary leadership provides direction to the team. The leader motivates, monitors the team, develops the team and manages the team. The skills, experience and knowledge of a team leader also has impact on team performance. A team manager has powers such as referral power, expert power, reward power, coercive power, and legitimate power.

A team manager with all these powers and conflict resolution techniques has to manage and resolve team conflicts and make a constructive conflict management, suitable for team performance. Usually, the effectiveness of team leadership is measured in terms of project success, team performance, and customer satisfaction. This is a qualitative dimension of a team.

To make a team successful and a performing team, none of these dimensions of teams can be ignored. All these dimensions are interlinked. Accordingly, team communication, team cohesion, team conflict and team performance is related or positively associated. Team processes such as communication, coordination, cooperation, cohesion have an impact on team effectiveness and performance. We have seen all these dimensions of teams and how to measure these dimensions and their relationships. Team work is very much required to execute complex projects.

16

Managing Dynamics in Teams

Teams are like the heart of any organization and with cooperation as well as teamwork anything is possible to achieve. The leader of the team should recognize that there is a discipline to study—the team dynamics—and the work of the team to know the blind spots and to operate as an effective team. Teamwork is one of the popular ways of organizational control.

There is a need to study team dynamics. How individuals behave in teams, how do they maintain relationships with their fellow team members, with their manager, how conflicts arise among team members and how to deal with tough team member etc. are discussed in this chapter.

16.1 Team Development Stages

Team orientation in organizations started in 1970s and has continued since then. Lot of research is going on to find the individuals behaviour in teams, teams' interaction, team dynamics etc. Every team in an organization undergoes a specific life cycle. A team undergoes stages of *forming, storming, norming* and *performing*. Another stage after performing is *adjourning*.

In the *forming* stage of team development, introduction among team members takes place. Everyone tries to behave formally with each other. There would not be any give and take relationship among team members. They will stick only to work relationship.

In the *storming* stage of team development, the differences among team members surface. Informal groups will form, from the formal team. There may be chances of informal leadership struggle also among the team members.

In the *norming* stage, team norms will be formed.

Everybody tries to follow those norms and guidelines. Slowly, give and take relationship starts in the team. The team forms their ground rules to follow.

In the *performing* stage, the team members know each other. They are comfortable with each other's behaviour and are considerate to other team members. There will be coordination and cooperation among the team members. Team productivity will be high in this stage. To reach this stage, a team must spend at least a year together.

A team reaches the *adjourning* stage after spending sometime in the performing stage. Here, in the adjourning stage, team members have contributed their part and are ready for their release from the team. They will go back to their respective vertical, once the project is over. This is the stage before team dissolves.

The team won't follow these stages sequentially. Because whenever a new team member joins the team or leader changes for the team, the team again enters into storming stage of team development. Hence, one should be careful when adding new team members to the team or while changing the team leadership in an organization. It is the responsibility of the current members to help new team members and get oriented with the team. How does the communication take place among team members will be discussed in the next section.

16.2 Managing Communications in the Team

It is the responsibility of a team leader to manage communication in the formal teams. He or she won't be having control over all the communication channels that exist in a team. However, they can control the information, which flows among the team members.

The communication process includes sender, receiver, medium of communication and channel of communication. In modern day organizations, where virtual teams exist in organizations, communication is taking place through email, fax, teleconferences, videoconferences, and webinars etc.

Different ways of communication channels are required which are based on the team members' location. Interpersonal as well as listening skills are a must for teamwork.

Written and oral communication is used among the team members based on the need and the complexity of the topic to be discussed. When the discussed topic is complex, it is better to use written communication. Informal discussions can be held orally. In a similar way, different forms of communication are required for formal and informal communication in the teams. It is better to find a common method of communication to understand the needs of team members and for better results. An organization, which encourages communication among team members, will have a high success rate in teamwork.

16.3 Virtual Teams

In virtual teams, team members are distributed geographically in different locations. They may be working in different time zones. These team members have a common goal. We can find virtual teams very commonly in the IT industry. With the onsite-offshore model and distributed development, team members are working in different countries in different time zones.

They collaborate and communicate using state of the art communication technologies such as teleconferencing, video conferencing, email, and data and voice communication technologies.

According to Lisa (1997), managing virtual teams means dealing with communication strategies, project management techniques, and human and social processes which takes care of the team. Virtual teams are of seven types. They are networked teams, parallel teams, project or product development teams, work or production teams, service teams, management teams, and action teams.

Advantages of virtual teams include easy cross-functional and cross-country communication, collaboration across companies and industries, and better intra-company and interdepartmental communication. For example, reduction in software product development time because of the time zone factor in different countries is another advantage of virtual teams.

16.4 Relationship among Team Members

Cooperation, rejection, denial, support, emotional attachment, like, dislike and attraction are some of the relationships that are possible among team members. Only team members are responsible for managing their relationships with their fellow team members.

In case any conflict arises between the team members, the leader can facilitate and resolve those conflicts. There is possibility of difference of opinion among team members as well in the team.

One should be responsible and careful when dealing with opposite sex team members. Attraction in initial stages should not turn into bitter relationships between them as the team progresses. There should be professional relationship among the opposite sex people in the team. If you observe, some of the companies encourage marriage between employees of an organization or team members. There are both positive and negative effects of it.

16.5 Relationship with a Manager

The behaviour of an individual team member in an organization is based on their relationship with their immediate supervisor. The way team members behave has a lot of influence on their leader or manager's relationship with them. If their relationship with their manager is good and cordial, they try to participate in team and organizational activities. If the team members are not having a good relationship with their manager, absenteeism, rejection, disintegration, and informal groups, occur in the teams. Sometimes, team members may challenge their team manager if their relationships are strained.

16.6 Working in Different Organizational Structures

There are different forms of organizational structures

available in the industry. These include functional, matrix and project oriented organizational structures. The reporting structure varies from one organization to another. In case of a matrix organization structure, a team member reports to two bosses, of which one is a functional manager and the other is a project manager. Again, matrix organization structures are of three types. They are weak matrix, balanced matrix and strong matrix organization structure.

Team members' interaction varies from one organization structure to another. In functional organization structure, the communication can be vertical and horizontal. In matrix kind of organization structure, even diagonal communication is possible in an organization.

Every team member will have a designation in the organization and role in the team. Here, the designation is different and role is different. The nine roles which the team members play are shaper, team worker, resource investigator, monitor evaluator, plant, completer-finisher, implementer, coordinator and specialist.

It is observed in the teams in an organization that one will be working as a supporter, one may be an executor, one may be a specialist at certain skills, or one may be a learner, etc. These people play different roles at different times. One won't be playing one role permanently. However, based on the situation, they change their roles.

The purpose of formal teams in an organization is to meet the organization's objectives. Every team will have an objective to achieve and team members work together to reach a common goal. There will be some team members whose objectives do not meet the organizational or team objectives.

If a team member is having objectives other than the team's objectives, it is better to keep him in the team whose objectives align with his personal objectives. If this is not possible, then it is better to advise him to find an organization whose objectives are similar to his objectives.

16.7 Self-managed Worker and Team

Usually, knowledge workers are self-managed workers. Managing knowledge workers is easier than managing non-knowledge workers. This is so because a knowledge worker is a self-managed worker and he can plan, as well as organize his work and coordinate with the other workers.

The manager plays an important role in managing self-managed workers as well, since motivating, directing and controlling the behaviours of team members still remain with the team manager. Hence, a manager plays a significant role in managing workers. In case of managing knowledge workers, the manager needs to have the domain specific knowledge as well to understand the team dynamics. The breed that will make the difference in service economy is the knowledge worker.

16.8 Managing Differences and Conflicts in Team

The manager is responsible for managing differences and conflicts in the team. In a team environment, there is possibility of differences and conflicts among team members. The manager has to respect the team members' differences. He or she should facilitate to remove the differences among team members. This is going to help in improving team productivity.

In a team environment, conflicts can exist among team members. There are several reasons for conflicts among team members. The reasons include schedules, priorities, costs, technical issues, resources, administrative issues, personality differences, benefits provided by the organization, etc.

When the conflicts arise, the manager has to resolve the conflicts by using techniques such as confrontation, smoothing, avoiding, compromise and forcing. The confrontation technique can create a win-win situation for the parties, who are in conflict. The confrontation with the help of facts and figures in hand creates a win-win situation. The forcing technique creates a win-lose situation.

16.9 Leadership in Teams

Generally, every formal team in an organization will have a team leader or manager assigned by it. However, in teams, there is possibility of the formation of informal groups and informal leaders. The more is the size of a formal team, the more these groups will form. Usually, the informal leaders in an organization will have the power gained through influencing skills.

The formal leader in an organization will have the powers such as legitimate, reward, penalty, expert and referral.

The cultural background of team members can also be the reason for differences or conflicts in the team environment. This is so because in industries like IT and pharmaceutical, people with diversified cultural background will be working together in teams. The manager should be in a position to welcome people from different cultures into the team. While developing team members, an organization should take into consideration, their diversity and work habits.

Some organizations believe that diversity improves productivity. The problem solving and decision-making process in the teams also have cultural influence. Diverse teams will also bring in a diversity of understanding and expectations about processes and team work in organizations. The objective in multicultural teams is to create an environment in which there is recognition for all team members. In multicultural teams, one of the strategies is to look at the problems as cultural differences rather than personality problems.

Most successful managers and leaders while dealing with problems in multicultural teams follow four strategies: adaptation, structural intervention, managerial intervention and exit.

16.10 Human Resource Skills Required for Managers

Recruiting, selection, induction, goal setting, performance evaluation, interviewing, communications management and conflict management skills are essential attributes of a team manager. A team manager's responsibilities vary from organization to organization. In some organizations, team managers are responsible for the deliverables only. They won't be having any people responsibility. In some other organizations, the team managers will have the responsibility of both the team members and the deliverables.

In product development environment, it is common to have interdisciplinary teams. In interdisciplinary teams, individual specialists from different disciplines or domains come together to work on a common goal. For example, in consumer durables manufacturing, electrical, mechanical, electronics, and software engineers, and marketing and sales executives come together to produce and market the products in an interdisciplinary way.

Similarly, while managing high performance teams, although it is difficult to retain the team members, yet retaining them can prove to be beneficial. Giving more responsibility to team members will enhance their sense of achievement. Describing the desired future of self-managing teams is difficult because it goes beyond the prevailing management and work paradigms and requires thinking about the vision of an organization.

In day-to-day life, sometimes team managers have to deal with tough team members. There should be a specific approach that a manager has to follow to deal with tough team members. Difficult behaviour can be extremely problematic to the workplace and can affect team productivity.

17

Recruitment Strategies of Indian IT Firms

With the increasing IT workforce in India, managing engineers and HR issues of this manpower are increasing day by day. With the growth of IT industry in India, there is a huge demand for skilled workers in Indian IT industry. Majority of Indian IT firms are recruiting in thousands. What these companies look for in a candidate while recruiting? What are their recruiting strategies? What are their sources of human talent? From where do these companies get the candidates? How do they interview candidates? What kind of selection methods they follow? The answers to these questions are furnished in this chapter.

17.1 Sources of Talent Pool

There are many sources of manpower to the IT companies in India. These sources are explained in detail below.

Usually, companies like Wipro and TCS consider internal candidates for new job openings. They have internal job boards established in their intranets. Whenever a new requirement comes up, they post a vacancy at their intranet and encourage internal candidates to apply for the job. If they do not find suitable candidates, they go on with selecting candidates from outside.

The preferred sources of candidates include current employees with employee referral program (ERP), customer referral, friends and relatives of the management and employees. Usually, the candidate selection rate is high, if a candidate comes from these preferred sources and there are more chances that the candidate stays with the organization for long time because he already knows the organizational culture through his known friends and relatives. If a candidate gets selected using the employee referral program, the employee gets remuneration for candidates selected from the employer. This remuneration varies from company to company. Also the employee morale improves in this case. One advantage with this employee referral program is that the employee mentors buddies with the selected candidates and introduces the company culture to the selected candidates because he already knows the candidates he is referring.

There are many other sources of candidates for the IT companies in India. They are newspaper advertisements, TV advertisements, radio advertisements and job fairs. These newspapers and other advertisements in media are useful for the collection of resumes in large scale and maintain a database of candidates for future purposes.

Job boards such as naukri.com, monster.com, jobsahead.com, and jobstreet.com are some of the sources of candidates for IT companies. The IT companies advertise in these job portals at affordable prices. Networking provided by sites such as LinkedIn, thesmarttechie.com, siliconindia.com are also some of the sources for good candidates for the IT companies.

Job fairs, conducted by the TimesJobs.com, Naukri.com and The Hindu, are also attracting young talent in India. Many IT companies are recruiting in these job fairs for entry-level programmer positions and making on the spot offers for the candidates. The external manpower consultants and engineering colleges and the universities campuses are the other sources for qualified candidates for the Indian IT companies.

17.2 Temporary to Permanent Employment

These days, the IT companies are hiring employees on contract basis. These companies want to have the trail run, that is, on job performance observance of the candidates before they take them on rolls. When companies need permanent employees, they interview the internal temporary employees available and make offers to them as permanent employees. For example, IBM India Software Lab, and Microsoft do this conversion of temporary workers into permanent employees, in India.

17.3 Recruiting Old or Retired Workers

Recruiting old and retired people is in considerable scale in IT-enabled services sector in India. However, the IT industry is yet to consider these candidates on large scale. These old and retired employees are a good source for domain and the industry expert positions, language editors and experts in specific areas. These employees have the knowledge and maturity to work in modern IT firms. They can learn new technologies like young engineers because they have sufficient time with them to learn newer things. The perception that an older worker is less productive than the younger one is false. Research indicates that analytical skills and numerical aptitude of human beings does not reduce with the age. It may stabilize after a certain age. A majority of older employees have better work ethics, and are more dependable and loyal (Art, 2006).

17.4 Targeting the Candidate

Usually, the Indian IT firms while recruiting the candidates, categorize them as a first step towards the recruitment activity. They categorize the candidates based on the size of the organization, number of needed resources and size of the candidate pool. They follow different strategies for candidates based on their categorization while recruiting them. The categorization of candidates can be based on their employment and achievement levels.

Candidates can be categorized as:

1. Disturbed candidate.
2. Undisturbed candidate.
3. Unemployed Candidate.
4. High achiever.
5. Average Performer.

Disturbed candidates are ready to accept the job offer immediately. They are easy to target and could be made to agree for the vacancy in hand easily. Undisturbed candidates are happy with the current job. However, if they get a call they may accept the offer. Unemployed candidates are actively looking for a job. Some of them may rush to accept the offer and some may not. This depends on their family or financial situation. High achievers are the ones who need to be tackled cautiously. It is difficult to make them agree for the job offer. They want a challenging role in a company to work for. Average performers are also comparatively easier to be moulded for a job offer.

IT firms categorize candidates accordingly and deal with each candidate separately. Based on the current and future vacancy in picture, these IT firms target the candidates. If the role is critical, they may target high achievers, and if it is not critical, they may target average performers. Indian IT firms have a difficult time in recruiting skilled manpower, and they find it even challenging to retain their existing trained employees.

17.5 Diversity in Workforce

Currently, many of the Indian IT companies are going global and setting up offices in Asia, Europe and America. For example, Satyam Computers has development centres in Dubai and China in addition to their headquarters in India. In fact, Satyam has multiple development centres in China. With the advent of the Global Delivery Model (GDM), Indian IT companies are becoming truly global by recruiting people from different countries. Within India itself, these software houses are recruiting people from different states and acclimatizing them with the diversity at workplace. TCS, Wipro, Infosys and Satyam are known examples for this kind of diversity. TCS has around 5,000 employees in APAC region including Japan and excluding India.

Many Indian IT organizations are moving towards workforce diversity. Organizations such as Infosys Technologies and Tata Consultancy Services are recruiting fresh graduates from reputed international universities abroad, training them in India and placing them in assignments across the world. This trend is picking up rapidly in Indian IT industry to attract talent available around the world. Companies like Wipro and TCS are recruiting and acquiring companies in Europe and Scandinavia to diversify their workforce. IBM has proved that workforce diversity is beneficial to organizational performance.

17.6 Selecting the Candidates

Different companies follow different techniques and tests in selecting the candidates. Usually, the IT firms go to the campuses and conduct written tests and interviews among the young engineers. The written tests include aptitude and analytical tests. The project leaders, project managers, senior management and HR team conduct face-to-face interviews. For lateral candidates, there will be two or three technical rounds and one HR round of interviews takes place. This interview process is typically a company-specific process.

After the resume screening, the candidate will be called for written test and interview. Recruitment in Infosys has been automated largely. Using a computer application, they were able to screen a million resumes and call 160,000 people to take part in the entry test.

17.7 Interviewer Strategies

During the interview, the interviewer should provide the right environment for the candidate to respond to the questions. In the interview only, the candidate will have a feel of the company. The interviewer should be careful while becoming tense or offensive in situations during the interview process. He should carefully respond to the contradictions. Initially, the interviewer should be given interviewing skills training. A majority of the Indian IT firms give interviewing skills training program to project leaders and project managers in their companies.

17.8 Recruitment Process Outsourcing (RPO)

RPO has been defined as, the outsourcing of specific

defined recruitment processes, performed in both centralized and decentralized applications, involving detailed service level agreements, with the vendor taking complete ownership of the processes of recruitment.

The trend in the HR field, in Indian IT industry, is moving towards outsourcing HR activities such as recruitment, payroll and candidate selection. For Example, Wipro BPO has outsourced recruitment process to MeritTrac. Similarly, other firms are also on their way to outsource the recruitment activities to HR consultancy firms in India. Already, a majority of the IT firms in India have many HR consultancy firms as their vendors in supplying the candidates as per their requirements. For example, iGate Corporation is a RPO provider. Till now, iGate was able to recruit more than 2,000 professionals on behalf of its clients.

IT companies are the early adapters of this RPO trend. At the same time, global RPO providers are also seriously evaluating the option of off-shoring their RPO work to countries such as India.

18

Software Programmer: The Management Perspective

When managing programmers, every project manager thinks about how to measure the performance of these programmers. Are there any benchmarks for doing that? How do other companies in the industry measure the performance of software engineers? What kind of parameters can be considered while evaluating the performance of software engineers? Answers to all these questions can be found in this chapter.

When a software engineer is recruited newly into the company, he/she undergoes the induction process followed by the enrolment process into the project. Once the organizational induction is over, the engineer is assigned to a specific project to work as a team member or in a specific role in the project. The project manager introduces the new team member to all the other team members in the project. Hereafter, the new engineer undergoes project induction and hands on training from the senior members of the team. As part of the formal process, the project manager sets the objectives for the new team member.

18.1 Setting Objectives

The objectives setting can be done formally or informally. In a majority of IT organizations, it is formal. The project manager sits with the new team member and sets the objectives for the coming one year or for the coming appraisal period. These objectives include the individual targets that the team members should achieve in the forthcoming year. Usually, these objectives will be inline with the organizational objectives and team objectives. They include the technical and non-technical objectives, which the team members should achieve in the coming appraisal period.

The technical objectives include the modules or the tasks that a team member has to execute in the project or the quality, and customer satisfaction levels that the team member should reach. The non-technical objectives include communication, leadership, and presentation skills as well as specific targets. This objective setting process takes place when a new member joins the team. The respective project manager documents these objectives and communicates them to the human resource department. A copy of the same will be with the team member as well.

18.2 Providing Training

The new team members will under go training in the organization and in the project. These trainings could be termed as on the job training and hands on training. The senior programmers or the designers in the team will train the new team members in project specific technologies and domains. Usually, every new engineer goes through project documentation and the training manuals of the project. The project manager makes sure that every new team member is properly trained in the relevant technologies and modules. Usually, the work assigned to a team member will be in sync with the objectives set by the project manager.

18.3 Evaluating Performance

Once the new team member spends one year or completes one appraisal period, it is time to evaluate his/her performance. The project manager will do this formal performance evaluation under the guidelines given by the HR department. Usually, the project manager evaluates the software engineer's technical and non-technical skills.

The non-technical skills such as communication, team play, and leadership skills are evaluated during the appraisal time. Other things like business etiquettes, ethical behaviour and mingling with organizational culture are also evaluated during the performance appraisal period.

Taking a poor performer out of the team may be more productive than adding a good performer to the team. The reasons for poor performance of a programmer include lack of job satisfaction, lack of identification, little belief that professional behaviour will result in rewards, and lack of sense of professionalism.

It is better to take the end results into consideration while measuring the performance of software engineers rather than considering the intermediate results. Some organizations even take the feedback from the customers while evaluating performance of the software engineers.

Technical skills such as designing, coding and testing of software engineers are evaluated during the performance appraisal time. There are many ways to measure the technical performance of software engineers. They include lines of code (LOC) per man month, number of function points (FP) implemented in a man month, time taken to implement a function point, customer satisfaction, number of bugs found for kilo lines of code, number of bugs fixed, time taken to fix a bug etc.

18.4 Measuring Lines of Code (LOC) Per Man Month

This is one way of measuring the performance of a software engineer. However, this may not be the correct measure to compare the performance of software engineers working in a team. It is not appropriate to say that the programmer who has written 10,000 lines of code is more productive than the programmer who has written 1,000 lines of code because the code of the later programmer may be very complex compared to the other. Or, the programmers might have used two different programming languages. If the programming languages are different, it cannot be measured by the number of lines of code. It is not known that the programmer who has written more number of lines of code might have written code, which may not be necessary. Hence, this may not be considered as an exact measure to evaluate the performance of software engineers.

18.5 Function Points Measure

Another way of measuring the performance of programmers is to measure the number of function points he/she has implemented in a man month or the time taken to implement a single function point. Because these function points are programming language independent, it can give a reasonable measure of a programmer's performance. To use this measure, there should be an expert function point estimator in the project team to estimate the function points accurately. In modern day organizations, separate project function point estimators do this activity.

18.6 Complexity Measure

Some of the organizations even measure the complexity of the code written by the individual programmers. This is useful to find out who has written the complex code in the project. Usually, the order of complexity of the algorithm can be found out by using different algorithm analysis and design techniques. It is the best practice to measure an individual programmer's performance by using these techniques.

18.7 Combination of Measures

As we know, the lines of code (LOC) per man month measure, cannot give the correct results to evaluate the performance of a programmer. It is advisable to have a combination of all these measures while evaluating the performance of software engineers. The other measures include number of use cases implemented in a man month, number of bugs found per kilo lines of code, number of bugs fixed, time taken to fix a bug, and backward traceability etc. Many organizations in the industry use the combination of all these measures while evaluating the performance of software engineers.

Defects injected during the design, need more time to fix than the defects injected during the coding time. Software

Engineering Institute (SEI) of Carnegie Mellon University (CMU) has defined a personal software process (PSP) to evaluate an individual programmer's performance. SEI has also defined a team software process (TSP) to evaluate the performance of teams as well. The personal software process takes into consideration the individual programmer and the time he/she has taken at each stage such as design, coding, and defect correction. Some of the metrics of PSP takes into consideration, planned versus actual estimates of tasks of the individual programmer.

During the performance appraisal, the non-technical skills of the programmer such as communication skills, comfortability with team, meeting organizational objectives, aligning with the organizational culture, meeting the organizational code of conduct, and the behavioural aspects are also evaluated. These aspects will have a significant weightage in the programmer's performance appraisal process.

Usually, the organizations are observing the engineers behaviour in teams because the teams rather than the individuals are executing many of the projects in organizations.

18.8 Leadership Training for Future Roles

Based on the performance appraisal of the programmer, training needs are identified for the individual programmer. Based on the interests of the engineer and project requirements, he or she will be given advanced technical training or managerial training. The programmers who took advanced technical training will become the future designers and architects and the programmers who took the managerial training will fill in for future project management roles in the organization.

Here, one important thing to be kept in mind is that a best programmer may not become a best manager. This is so because, a project manager requires an entirely different skill set which includes decision-making, negotiation, problem solving, leadership, conflict resolution, and quantitative, conceptual and communication skills.

18.9 Career Paths for Programmers

The programmers can take the path of either management or architecture/design path. Based on the programmer's interests, he or she can get trained towards that direction. Usually, experienced programmers become designers or technical leads for the product. Those who are interested in communication and team leading roles may become project leaders and project managers in the organization.

If a programmer chooses the managerial path, he can grow to the role of project, program, or portfolio manager or director (engineering) and VP positions in the organization. If he or she chooses the technical path, they can become technical leader, designer, architect and chief architect for the product.

The programmers can pursue senior technical positions, business and system analysis positions, project management positions and management roles. Making the shift to management can be done on the job by taking greater responsibilities, polishing problem-solving skills and using creativity at workplace.

Some companies assume that the next position to a programmer is the project manager without even taking the consent and interest of the programmer into account. Project management roles need special skills other than programming skills. Those skills include communication, presentation, leadership, problem solving, decision-making, negotiation, and conceptual skills.

A programmer can become a project manager by taking up wider responsibilities and leading other team members in the team. He needs to have an understanding of project, scope, time, cost, quality, human resources, communications, risk and procurement management techniques and tools. He needs to have the knowledge of the project management areas mentioned above.

18.10 Moving Across Projects

Once the programmer spends sometime in one project, he/she will be moved to another project, based on the project completion, or needs of other important projects within the organization. He/she can move across the domains or across the technologies or across the verticals.

Usually, the senior project managers, program and resource managers move team members across the projects based on the organizational requirements and the team member's needs or interests.

Based on the programmers' performance appraisal, promotions, demotions and transfers take place in the organization. The promotions can be towards more technical roles or towards managerial roles. If the organization feels that the programmer's performance is not meeting the requirements of the project, they can even move him to a low level technical role in other projects or even some disciplinary action can be taken.

There are some industry standards evolved in measuring the organizational performance and individual performance. CMMI and PCMM come under those standards used to evaluate the maturity of the processes in an organization. These models were developed by the Software Engineering Institute (SEI) at Carnegie Mellon University. Explanation of these two models follows.

18.11 Capability Maturity Model Integration (CMMI)

The Software Engineering Institute (SEI) at Carnegie Mellon University issues the CMMI standards. Capability Maturity Model Integration is a process improvement approach, which provides organizations with essential elements of effective processes. It can be applied to projects, departments or to the entire organization. CMMI helps in integrating the organizational functions with the quality processes and gives guidance as well as sets goals for quality processes.

One of the benefits of CMMI is that more linking is possible between engineering activities and organizational business objectives. It also fully complies with relevant ISO standards. The different levels of CMMI include initial, managed, defined, quantitatively managed, and optimizing. CMMI is being adopted across Americas, Europe, Asia, Australia and Africa.

18.12 People Capability Maturity Model (PCMM)

People Capability Maturity model (PCMM) is also from SEI. It focuses on continuous improvement and development of human aspects of the organization. There are different maturity levels defined in PCMM, which deal with the human resources, and organization development related aspects. PCMM gives a framework, which helps the organizations in addressing the critical people issues.

More research is needed in order to find out the benchmarks for evaluating the performance of software engineers. Majority of modern organizations use a combination of different measures. There is scope for the development of standards in measuring the performance of programmers. As a team player, both the technical and soft skills of the programmer together make him/her a good contributor to the project. Hence, there should be good and reasonable measures to evaluate the performance of software engineers working in the industry. With the application of PCMM frameworks, the organizations can handle the people issues in a more matured way.

19

Teamwork in Software Organizations

The Indian IT job market is picking up and young engineers are getting offers from reputed IT firms. The outside world might be wondering about the success of Indian IT industry and its delivery and business models. The hidden strength behind this success is the Indian software development teams. It is the team orientation, delivery approach, processes, and customer focus which is giving repeat customers to Indian IT organizations. Thus, this chapter will focus on Indian software teams.

19.1 Team Organization

Basically, team orientation in organizations has come into existence since the studies of Fredric Taylor's scientific management. However, this has been picked up aggressively in multinational organizations since 1970s. Currently, more than 2/3rd of the Fortune 500 organizations are delivering their products and services to customers using teams. Industries such as hardware, software, pharmaceutical, construction, healthcare, manufacturing and telecom are extensively using teams not only in product development but also in other business functions such as marketing, HR, and finance.

There exist different types of teams in an organization. They are *project teams, work teams, parallel teams*, and *management teams*. Usually, one can find *project teams* in software, hardware and telecom companies. These teams have specific objectives to be achieved in a specified time limit with the given budget and acceptable quality by the customer. One can find *work teams* in manufacturing industries and where assembly line work goes on. *Parallel teams* can be found in research areas such as drug discovery and biotechnology areas, and also in some IT organizations. Top *management team* consists of the C-level executives such as CEO, COO, CMO, CTO, and CIO. They work as a team in most of the multinational organizations.

19.2 Characteristics of Teams

Team is a collection of people working together with complementary skills and for a common purpose and objective. Every team in an organization has got an objective to achieve. For example, project teams work towards the project end product, result or service.

A team may consist of individuals with varied experience levels, different gender, age, different skill set, different educational and organizational backgrounds, different race, religion, and different ethnic backgrounds.

All team members work towards the team objective under the leadership of a team leader. Mutual trust, cooperation, cohesion, respect for others, cultural sensitivity, maturity, and support for others, safety for team participation, having team vision, task orientation, and support for productive environment and having team norms and ground rules are some of the characteristics of teams in organizations.

The members in high performance teams have certain special characteristics. They include collective accountability, collective ownership, mutual trust, support for other team members' development and welfare, superior customer orientation, task orientation, having great team vision, situational group leadership, group decision-making, and respect for others' culture, language, region and religion.

19.3 Teams in Software Organizations

One can find many types of teams in software organizations. They are: development teams, support teams, testing teams, maintenance teams, quality teams and disaster recovery teams.

As is known, *development teams* develop the product or

solutions, based on customer requirements or any standard specifications. These development projects have team members and project manager to work on the project. They have fixed time limit to deliver a project product. These teams are given fixed budget and time and desired quality limits. It is very rare to find a project team with unlimited time and money allotted to it. These project development teams focus on gathering, analysis, designing the solution, and coding.

Support teams in software organizations respond to customer calls and queries. Technical support can be provided at different levels such as Level 1, 2, and 3. Level 1, 2, and 3 support teams have specified time limits to respond to customer queries. If the support team is not able to solve a customer technical problem, it escalates the issue and sends it to the development team. Or some of the customer problems may result into defects or bugs or new features of a product.

Testing teams in software organizations usually take care of system testing and integration testing of the project product. Usually, test teams are led by a test manager. Writing test cases, executing test cases, reporting defects and tracking defects are the main activities of the test teams. Once a product build happens, development team hands over the pre-tested product to the test team. Test team check the product and gives the necessary test summary reports and test statistics.

Maintenance teams in software organizations mainly does fixing of bugs and in some cases developing new features for the product. In some organizations, development team itself handles the product maintenance activities. Maintenance teams may involve in releasing fix packs or patches to the product.

Quality teams in software organizations take care of process related quality assurance activities. They ensure that the intermediate project deliverables are reviewed and meet organizational quality standards. They help in conducting reviews of deliverables such as design documents and source code and they conduct quarterly and periodic quality audits. Quality team does all the internal process related activities to ensure the delivery of a quality product to the customer.

In current days, there are other types of teams in software organizations such as design teams, requirements gathering teams, reengineering teams, product innovation teams, R&D teams and disaster recovery teams. Disaster recovery teams in software organizations handle cases such as data loss, hard disk failure and network failure, etc.

All these teams do not work in an isolated environment. They work in collaboration and cooperation with each other. Coordination between these teams should be there in meeting the customer requirements. In some cases, the output of one team becomes the input of another team. For example, development team's output viz. the product build, is the input for the test team.

19.4 Managing Software Teams

According to management philosophy, a knowledge worker is self-managing and needs little supervision. Same thing applies to software engineers. However, based on the complexity of work, software teams need to be motivated and brought into track if there are any disturbances in the team. This is due to the possibility of conflicts arising between team members, that is, intra-group and inter-group conflicts in software organizations. The reasons for these conflicts can be any shared resources between the teams, profit sharing, costs, administrative issues, project priorities and project dependencies across multiple teams. The program manager has to resolve all these conflicts among the project teams.

To motivate the software teams in an organization, there should be proper reward and recognition system in place, training needs of the teams should be identified, hardware and software resources need to be provided, and right environment has to be provided to the teams to make them productive. Senior management has to set the objectives for each project team and monitor their respective progress. They have to communicate and handle the dependencies between the project teams.

19.5 How to Evaluate Performance of Software Teams?

Software organizations are too much worried about how to improve individual as well as team productivity; how to compare one team with another team to decide whether to continue the team in the organization or to dissolve the team. Many researchers have found different ways of measuring software development team productivity. Those measures include KLOCs, function points, object points or use case points implemented per man hour.

Among all these, function points (FP) measure is the prominent one because it is programming language independent. A team implementing 20 FPs in one man month is more productive than a team implementing 15 FPs in one man month. However, this kind of comparison in KLOCs cannot be done between teams if the programming language is different. *Productivity* is the number of units produced per unit of input time.

Similarly, test teams' productivity can be compared by number of test cases executed per unit of time. Similarly, support teams' productivity can be compared by number of customer requests or calls attended during a specified time by the competing teams. These are basically *quantitative* measures. However, *qualitative* measures such as customer satisfaction, project product or service quality, stakeholder satisfaction, or top management satisfaction levels can be used for evaluating performance of different teams in software organizations. Sometimes, audits (both internal and external) and reviews are also used as performance measure instruments for software teams.

Based on the team's performance appraisal, top management should take corrective actions. There are many factors affecting the productivity and performance of software teams in the Indian scenario. These factors include selection of hardware, software tools, customer behaviour, project manager behaviour, selection of programming language, socio- economic, political and legal environment, lack of specific technical skills, experience and competency of engineers, top management commitment and support, organizational culture, organizational climate, team climate and organizational politics.

As one famous saying goes, "unless you measure, you cannot improve upon it". Thus, one can definitely evaluate the productivity of software teams in the organization and can compare and take necessary actions on the teams based on organizational needs, strategy and vision.

Using these measures, organizations can strive for continuous improvement and make the teams more productive.

19.6 Fostering Productivity in Team Work

Usually, in IT organizations, projects are executed by the teams. The teams behave differently based on the stage in which the team is currently placed. What are the phases involved in team development? How team members behave in teams during these phases? How the teams are formed? How the teams are dissolved? These are the common questions a project manager usually encounters. If we see, there are different phases a team undergoes in an organization. The phases and the challenges the teams face, are explained below.

19.6.1 Forming: It is the phase in which team members are introduced to each other. One will come to know about each other's name, experience, background, etc. In this phase, team members work independently. The leader should be directing the team in this phase.

19.6.2 Storming: In storming stage, team members start communicating with each other. They put forward their thoughts in team meetings. Everybody wants to win the discussion. This is a very crucial stage in team development.

19.6.3 Norming: In this phase of team development, team members are considerate to each other. They will come to know about each other. They start trying to respect each others points. In this stage of team formation, team just starts producing results. The leader should be participative in style in this stage of team development.

19.6.4 Performing: In performing stage, the team really works as a team. The decisions are collectively taken by the team. The decisions made are the team decisions rather than the manager's decisions. To reach this stage, the team has to spend few years together. You observe these kinds of performing teams in US in MNCs such as IBM, HP and Microsoft. The teams work together for years. Resultantly, the team performance will be very effective and very high. Team members understand the emotions of each other very well in this stage. The role of the leader in this stage should be a participative one.

19.6.5 Mourning: In this stage of team development, the team completes the tasks and the team is dissolved. The team members are relocated to new teams.

These steps are followed when the team is led by a single leader throughout the project. Whenever leader changes, the team again enters into storming stage at some point of time. This should be the main area of concentration for senior management when they are changing project leaders frequently.

19.7 Team Development

The team members are to be mentored by the leader or some experienced person in the organization during their stay in the project. The product development teams in IT MNCs definitely undergo all these phases of team development. This is so because the product development and maintenance teams stay longer together than the services teams. In product development teams, the team members should definitely know about each other very well. Cooperation and coordination should be there among team members in teams. An ideal manager can handle six to eight team members as his direct reportees. Hence, the services and product development companies should keep this in mind and form the teams accordingly. If the manager has more than eight team members then it is better to have layers in the reporting structure. This helps the manager in concentrating on the deliverables and can handle people issues effectively.

Hence, for choosing the product development teams, one should think for the long-term. The team members should be stable and should know each other very well. If we have stable teams, it is easy to deliver quality products to the customers.

19.8 Need for High Performance Teams in Indian IT Industry

Indian IT and BPM industry's revenue was estimated at around US$ 191 billion in 2019-2020, growing at a rate of 7.7 percent y-o-y basis. It is estimated to reach US$ 350 billion by 2025. As on December 31, 2019, total number of employees grew to 1.02 million cumulatively for four Indian IT majors including TCS, Infosys, Wipro, HCL Tech. Additionally, the Indian IT industry employed 205,000 new hires and had 884,000 digitally skilled talent in 2019.

Hence, there is need to think about how we are working and delivering solutions to the customers in this industry. How are we organizing and executing inside the organization to provide solutions and timely response to customer queries and problems.

Traditionally, organizations have given much importance to individual contributions. Because of the growing nature of complexity and inherent benefits of achieving parallelism and reduced response time to customer problems, work teams came into the organization for executing the projects. This research on teams started with the Fredric Taylor's scientific experiments on workers in manufacturing and assembly line plants. Slowly, this team orientation has come to knowledge-based industries such as IT, biotechnology, pharmaceutical and management consulting. Currently, more than 80 percent of Fortune 500 companies are executing their projects and achieving their organizational objectives using work teams inside their organizations.

A team is a collection of individuals working towards a common organizational goal. These days, there are many forms of teams. There are traditionally *collocated teams* in organizations. These teams stay at the same geographic location or office. There is one more concept known as *war room*. If a team is developing a complex product, all the team members of that team sit in the same room. This room is known as the war room. Also, there are distributed teams such as *virtual teams*. These teams are distributed geographically across different locations. Sometimes, virtual teams may be spread across different countries and continents.

Virtual teams use technology to the maximum extent for team communication purposes. They use email, video conferences, teleconferences, and web conferences extensively. These team members might not have seen each other physically before the start or during the project. However, they all work towards a common goal and develop a product. Indian IT firms like TCS, Infosys, Wipro, and HCL use these kinds of teams very extensively. In high technology and product development companies such as Intel, Nokia, IBM, HP, SUN, and Microsoft one can find war rooms quite frequently.

Modern day objective of these IT firms is to achieve more productivity using project teams. What western organizations are looking for is the high performance in work teams. You find *high performance teams* in US in organizations like IBM, Microsoft, HP and Motorola. The high performance teams exceed organizational expectations and increase the revenues and reduce costs for the organizations.

There are different schools of thought for a team to become a high performance team. Usually, according to Tuckman's theory, a team becomes a performing team once it crosses stages such as forming, storming, and norming. Later, the team becomes a performing team. A team becomes a high performance team once it crosses the stages of work group, pseudo team, potential team and real team.

19.9 Characteristics of High Performance Teams

High performance teams in organizations exhibit certain characteristics. High performance teams have common purpose, objective, and goal. Team members in high performance teams exhibit mutual trust and mutual respect. There is personal commitment from team member towards the project and the organization. Team members exhibit interpersonal commitment as well. They care for the growth and well-being of the fellow team members. There is shared leadership in the team. Whoever is known and confident in that situation, he or she takes care of the situation.

There is group decision-making in the team. They collectively solve the problems. They welcome conflicts and manage conflicts effectively. Team members communicate effectively in the team. Team members feel accountability and they also exhibit mutual accountability in the project. They speak openly and share their concerns with others. Instead of reporting to the team leader, they update fellow team members and take their consent and approvals frequently. They feel that they belong to the team. Also, the high performance teams look to satisfy all the stakeholders in the project. Usually, the team members in high performance teams will have complementary skills.

Like this, these are the some of the characteristics high performance teams, exhibit in an organization. This is possible with the kind of organizational climate and trust among the team members. This can be achieved through long-term association of team members with complementary skills in the project. IT Organizations like IBM and Motorola have experimented and had success with high performance teams.

19.10 The Indian Scenario

Mostly, Indian IT firms are in software services sector. The component of product development is very small compared to services provided to the customers. Hence, the teams working in these firms are having relatively less project durations. There is not much scope for the team members to build trust with the fellow team members. By the time a team member becomes comfortable with a fellow team member, the project is nearing closure and he/she will move on to another project team.

Hence, there is need for the Indian IT firms to look at creating high performance teams for long-term sustainability. Without mutual trust, a team cannot reach high performance levels. Once you have high performance teams in an organization, the senior management can face customers with improved confidence. Considering the inherent benefits, it is time for the Indian IT industry to go for high performance teams which would improve the organization's confidence level and also reduce the customer response time.

20

Project Stakeholders and Technology

There are many stakeholders which interact with a project manager in his day-to-day activities. All these stakeholders are interested in selected information about the project. The project manager has to monitor what information is flowing to which stakeholder. In this chapter, we will see how stakeholders can affect a project manager in his day-to-day activities and what role they play with respect to a certain project. All these stakeholders are important because they are affected by the success or failure of a project.

The main stakeholders who interact with the project manager are team members, project sponsor, senior management, quality team, support team, vendors, contractors, customers, users, marketing team, and any other stakeholders affected by the outcome of the project.

20.1 Team Members

They are also known as project team. They are the people directly reporting to the project manager. Definitely, they interact with the project manager on a continuous basis. A project manager is involved in selecting the team, recruiting the team, setting of objectives, and performance appraisal of the team. He delegates the work to the team members. He monitors and controls the progress of the work.

20.1.1 Project Sponsor: A project sponsor is interested in the progress of the project. He is interested in the success of the project. Because he is the person who invests money for the project, definitely he would like to interact with the project manager on regular intervals. He will suggest the manager in case of a schedule overrun and cost overrun, whether to continue with the project or close the same.

20.1.2 Senior Management: These people are interested in the review of the project. Usually, the senior management reviews meetings happening in the organization. In these meetings, the project manager highlights the progress of the project with the help of project metrics. Senior management is interested in details such as efforts spent, defects statistics, productivity, etc. All these details have to be provided by the project manager in senior management review meetings. He may have to tell his resource acquisition plans as well.

20.1.3 Quality Team: These are the people who will give green signal to release the product or the result of the project. Quality control is done by the quality team. Also, a project manager has a lot of control in the quality assurance stage. Definitely the quality people are in constant touch with the project manager in dealing with the process related matters. The quality people involve the project manager in quality audits and quality assurance activities.

20.1.4 Support Team: Once the product is released into the market, the support team work starts from there. The product engineering team hands over the product to the support team when the release happens. Once the product release happens, the support team is responsible in responding to customer queries. These support people take over the knowledge transfer from the product engineering team and the project manager. That's how support team interacts with the project manager. Also, in case the support team is not able to handle customer queries, it will be forwarded to the project manager. Accordingly, the project manager has to respond to the customer queries with the help of his engineering team.

20.1.5 Vendors: Vendors are the people who take some chunk of work from the performing organization. The project manager selects the vendors based on vendor selection criteria. Once the vendors are selected, they are given work on contract basis or time and material basis.

20.1.6 Contractors: These are the people who are stationed at the project manager's location and execute the project. Usually, the project manager pays to these contractors on hourly or daily basis. They work at the performing organization for a fixed time period based on their contract with the performing organization.

20.1.7 Customers: Definitely, the project manager will be communicating with the customers regularly. The customer is interested in weekly and monthly status reports, schedule and cost overruns. The customer has the authority to continue or stop the project.

20.1.8 Users: Users are the people who interact with the systems developed by the project teams. Definitely, user feedback is an input for the project manager. In some cases, users are within the organization or in some cases the users may be outside the performing organization. User feedback is very important in framing the requirements.

20.1.9 Marketing Team: These are the people who interact with the customers and then provide feedback to the project manager. These people act as an interface between a customer and the project manager in some organizations. In product-oriented companies, usually product features are driven by the customer needs, wants and expectations. Hence, these are gathered by the marketing team and given to the project manager.

20.1.10 Other Stakeholders: There can be many other stakeholders for projects. For example, families of the employees can be stakeholders for some projects. The general public may be stakeholders for an environment related project. Hence, identification of stakeholders is an important activity that a project manager needs to concentrate on. This is a continuous process.

20.2 People Side of Project Management

Team work is the backbone for the success of any project these days. Starting from recruitment of the project team members until releasing the team members from the project, it is the project manager who manages the team and the project.

If the team size is very big, there will be a project management team to manage project and team members. The project manager recruits team members, trains them, develops them, and manages them. It is the project manager's responsibility to plan the communications in the project. Everybody in the project may not need all the information in the project. It is the project manager who categorizes the information and distributes it to the desired stakeholders. This below sections will explain the steps related to the people side of project management in an organization.

20.2.1 Human Resource Planning: The project manager is responsible for planning human resources for the project. Usually, projects require maximum number of people during its peak time and minimum number of people during the initiation and closing times. A project manager should try to utilize the available resources and he should try to acquire the resources, if needed. He can make use of resource graphs. While assigning the team members to the projects, it is advisable to assign team members based on their skill set and interests. For example, young engineers may like to work in advanced technologies and experienced resources may like to stick to their legacy technologies. Taking their interests into consideration reduces the attrition rate in the project.

20.2.2 Acquire Team Members: The project manager employs many techniques to acquire the project team. The main technique is the negotiation. He negotiates with the fellow project/line managers to acquire key team members. Sometimes, team members will be pre-assigned. Some highly skilled resources are very expensive and their availability is very rare. In this kind of scenario, the project manager should plan ahead and try to get highly skilled resources needed for the project. The reputation of the team members is related to the success of the project. If the team members think that the project is not going to be successful, they try to exit from the project. The project manager should handle this situation delicately. In acquiring team members, he should choose those team members who meet the requisite expectations.

20.2.3 Develop Team Members: It is the project manager who cares for the welfare of the team members. He has formal, reward, punish, referral and expert powers to use on the team members. The expert power is a powerful tool sometimes. With knowledge and technical skills, the project manager can gain expert power and can use it on the team. While acquiring team members, a project manager should assess the technical skills of the team members. He should assess the desired skills and if there is any gap, the project manager should provide training to the team members.

20.2.4 Mentoring: Providing mentors to the young engineers is very important in grooming their careers. These days MNCs like Siemens and IBM are providing mentors to all employees when they join the company. These mentors are very experienced in their field and will be able to guide young engineers in their technical and non-technical issues.

20.3 How to Manage Team Members?

It is a best practice to provide continuous feedback on the performance to the team members. Many organizations are taking 360 degree feedback for their employees in their performance appraisals. It is better to set objectives for team members whenever a new team member joins the team or at the beginning of the appraisal period. Best practice is to measure the performance against the objectives set earlier. It is better to keep all the performance measurement factors in quantitative terms rather than keeping them in qualitative terms.

It is the project manager's responsibility to release the team whenever the work is complete. If there exists conflict among the team members, the project manager should be adept to handle and resolve the same. In these kinds of situations, confrontation is the best conflict resolution technique a project manager can use. Other conflict resolution techniques include smoothing, compromising, withdrawal and forcing. The main reason for the conflict among team members is the schedules.

Other reasons include cost, technical issues, resources, priorities, and personality problems. When conflict occurs, the project manager should try to resolve the conflict using any of these conflict resolution techniques.

A project manager can manage the communications in the project. But he is not having control over the all existing communication channels in the team. If the project consists of 'n' number of team members, there exists n * (n-1) number of communication channels in the project. Hence, the project manager does not have time to control all these communication channels. However, he can control the information being passed to all the team members in the project.

The project manager should identify what information is to be distributed to whom. Once this identification is over, he can then distribute the information to the stakeholders on timely basis. He should note down all needs, wants and expectations of the stakeholders.

The project status information should reach all the stakeholders according to the communication plan. The project manager has to manage the stakeholders effectively. If there is any problem with a stakeholder, the project manager has to meet with that stakeholder for an open discussion.

20.4 Best Practices for Project Management

There are few best practices in the IT industry which every firm follows. Because of the nature of the technical work, there is a lot of scope for innovation in the products and processes of software development. This section will explain the best practices followed by well-known IT firms. Best practices in project management, software development methodologies, software development processes, recruitment, selection, reward and recognition system, training and environment are explained below.

Recruitment is the first step in any organization. Project inception also starts with recruitment of team members and the project manager. Usually, while recruiting employees, organizations take utmost care in their recruitment process. Particularly, the small and medium enterprises (SMEs) go for known resources for getting the best talent.

20.5 Best Practices for Selection

Selection of suitable candidates is the next step in recruitment. Different companies use different approaches for the selection of candidates for their organization. The best practices among the selection methods include case based approach, and aptitude tests. For example, Microsoft's case based approach for recruiting programmers and architects is widely known. Other companies such as TCS and Infosys conduct analytical tests for fresh graduates during the campus interviews. Some companies such as Computer Associates and Sasken conduct technical tests such as C++ and Java for the entry-level programmer positions.

Using these techniques, programmers and technical leads are recruited into the team. Product development companies conduct tests on specific programming language skills in software industry. Because their products are being developed in specific technologies, they want gurus in that technology only. However, software services organizations recruit people with some average technical skills having good analytical and numerical aptitudes, so that they can train them in any technology and depute them in the designated project. Moving these programmers across the projects and verticals becomes easier for the software services firms.

While selecting candidates for the project, program and delivery manager positions, companies usually look at their stability in the current organizations, and while conducting selection tests, they may resort to psychometric tests for the candidates. Using these tests, the companies test the confidence level, maturity and leadership skills of the candidate. These kinds of tests are very common in advanced countries such as USA and UK for appointing candidates for the managerial roles.

20.6 Best Practices for Performance Appraisals

Every software organization conducts performance appraisals of their engineers on a periodic basis. The best practice is to do the job conformance appraisal after six months to one year of the candidate's joining date. Many IT firms have this practice of confirmation appraisals in their organizations. It is better to have self-appraisal, supervisor's appraisal and a reviewer comments for each employee's performance appraisal.

Usually, rating scale method is followed in the appraisal forms. It is better to appraise the communication, presentation skills of the engineer in addition to the technical skills. While appraising project, program and delivery managers, it is their managerial skills, which needs to be appraised. It is their project and people management skills, which needs to be evaluated for the appraisal period.

20.7 Best Practices in Project Development Process

Indian software firms are well known for their quality consciousness. Majority of the Indian software firms have SEI-CMMi or ISO 9001 certifications or both. These processes help in the quality assurance process for any project. Majority of the organizations are trying for continuous improvement in their process capabilities. For example, Wipro, Infosys and TCS are rated at SEI-CMMi level 5. Wipro is following six-sigma quality process in some of its processes. Rational's Unified Process (RUP) is also a known process followed in software projects.

Not only the software or manufacturing processes are being followed for the quality assurance activities but also capabilities like project management are being assessed and measured. For example, Project Management Institute's (PMI, USA), Organizational Project Management Maturity Model (OPM3) is useful for assessing and measuring the project management maturity in the organization. Some of the IT firms in US are going for this kind of project management maturity assessment.

Some of the companies follow PRINCE 2 (Projects IN Controlled Environment) methodology for project management in their projects. PRINCE is widely used in Europe and UK. PMI, USA's PMBOK (Project Management Body of Knowledge) is widely used across the world.

Many of the software houses are encouraging their employees to undergo PMI-PMP (Project Management Professional) certification. This is because the western based customers are insisting on PMP qualified project managers from the performing organizations. PMI also came up with a certification for Program Management (PgMP).

20.8 Best Practices for Software Development Methodologies

There are some of the best practices being followed in the software companies in using specific software development methodologies. Some of those methodologies are Agile, Extreme programming and Scrum methodologies. Some of the firms use Object Management Group's (OMG) Unified Modelling Language (UML) as their project design methodology.

Another best practice is to conduct peer reviews and/or external (to team) reviews for each deliverable in the software development life cycle. This definitely improves the quality of the deliverable. Collective responsibility and incremental deliverables are some of the upcoming concepts and practices in the industry.

For any new organization, there is no point in reinventing the wheel for basic operations. Hence, it can follow some of the best practices followed in the industry. Usually, there is scope for improvement and innovation in organizational operations. Hence, software organizations can excel in their operations with the help of best industry practices, innovation and creativity.

20.9 Skills versus Experience

Many people have made successful careers in the IT industry without a computer science background. They have gained good roles in organisations, based on their exposure and experience. You no longer need to go through a formal professional course to enter the IT industry. Anyone with enough exposure to computers and software can get a firm enough hold in the IT industry. In fact, because of the lack of talented B.Tech and MCAs, companies like Wipro and Infosys are recruiting B.Sc graduates.

Software development requires much innovation and creativity. Software development is more an art than a science. Good analytical skills and logical thinking capabilities are a prerequisite. Many successful programmers in the IT industry globally have not had a formal computer science education. Many started out with small software training programs. Many IT companies provide state-of-the-art technology on-the-job training. Software companies invest a lot in technical and managerial training programs.

'Time to Retire the Retirement'—an article published in the March 2004 issue of *Harvard Business Review* focused on the emerging role of youth in the industry. According to the article, many companies are providing training to young people. All training programs are prepared keeping the young people in mind. However, sometimes these young trainees may end up working for some other company. With this, the company's investment becomes waste. Research says that mature workforce is more stable than the young workforce. So, it may be wise for companies to also consider the relatively older workforce when they plan training and development programs.

20.10 Tapping Managerial Talents

Many software engineers are interested to work as software consultants. Now-a-days, very few software engineers are interested to take up management positions. There are a lot of opportunities in the project management, program management and operations management areas in IT industry.

Companies like Wipro, Infosys and TCS are investing a lot on technical training programs. The software services companies are mostly concentrating on updating their employees with the state-of-the art technologies. They want to do new projects with latest technologies for their clients. They are maintaining an in-house technical knowledge base.

Indian IT companies should concentrate on producing global technology managers for the 21st century. They should invest more on providing management training for the young engineers to make them future project managers.

In the present industry scenario, project management is dominated by the western world. Indian software engineers are doing the lower-end technical work. They should move up the value chain and lead the projects. Indian software companies should recognize the young management potential in their employees and should provide good management education to those employees.

They should maintain an in-house management knowledge base and train their employees with case studies based approach. Most of the Indian IT services companies should provide world class training to their managers.

A majority of Indian IT companies sponsor their employees for advanced technology programs like Master of Science (MS) in computer science. In the same way, these companies should encourage their employees to do MBA. Integration of technology with management education has well known advantages for the industry. For example, Wipro sponsors their employees for the MS program in computer science. Wipro has tie-up with BITS, Pilani and Illinois Institute of Technology (IIT), USA. These universities provide advanced computer education to Wipro employees.

20.11 Impact of Advanced Technologies on HR Function

Technologies are changing faster than the speed at which organizations can grasp. In the IT industry, the HR function is facing many changes and challenges because of the advanced and high technologies. Technologies such as cloud computing, mobile computing, pervasive computing, social technologies, big data and analytics are changing the face of HR function in IT organizations. The traditional recruitment and training functions are undergoing a drastic change. These technologies are not only changing the business models but also impacting the organizational culture, organizational learning, organizational structures, organizational design, intellectual property, information security and knowledge management.

20.11.1 Cloud Computing: Using cloud computing, the start-up organizations can start their operations from day one itself. Cloud is a logical network of computers with virtualization and storage facilities which provides infrastructure, platforms and software. Clouds can be deployed in four forms. They are public clouds, private clouds, community clouds and hybrid clouds.

Public clouds are accessible over the internet. With membership, one can access public clouds. Cloud providers own and operate public clouds. With public clouds such as Amazon Elastic Cloud availability, organizations need not worry about the infrastructure. This feature is making the infrastructure teams in the organization redundant because these facilities are being provided by the cloud providers themselves. HR functions going behind the infrastructure experts, is going to be decided by the usage of the clouds in an organization.

Private clouds, however, are going to create some infrastructure roles in the organization, if the organization itself owns and operates a private cloud. Private cloud is a cloud meant for an organization. It can be a part of an enterprise network. Another deployment model is outsourcing the private cloud to third party provider. This also makes the infrastructure team in the organization redundant. Hence, there is a challenge for HR team in IT organizations. Community cloud is meant for a group of organizations. In case of community clouds, the specific group of organizations have to share the responsibility of owning and operating the cloud with shared human resources to operate it.

20.11.2 Mobile Computing: Mobile computing is changing the face of customer support, financial services, customer relationships and employee relationships. Yahoo has given their managers smart phones. 2G, 3G and 4G are picking up in mobile area. Mobile devices are growing at a fast rate in developing countries such as India. Smartphones are changing the face of retail, governance, education and healthcare across the world. Maintaining a single source of contact for customers is a challenge today. Some companies are developing mobile apps for employee self-service. Organizations are going mobile for operations in 24x7 model and for productivity reasons. Tracking the communication and managing mobile culture are major challenges for HR executives in the organizations. These are sometimes disrupting the important meetings and discussions as well in the organizations.

20.11.3 Pervasive Computing: Pervasive computing is embedding microprocessors in day-to-day devices and accessories so that the devices become smart and communicate with each other. The current trend is 'internet of things' in some parts of the developed world. It is yet to reach the developing world. For example, one can turn on thermostat at home while reaching the home from a distant radius remotely. A car can drive on its own and park itself. There are connected homes in the world. There are smart watches and smart shoes as well with embedded processors in it. These all have been successfully tried in parts of the world. Japan's Honda would like to make zero human loss in accidents involving their cars by 2050. These are all the technological developments going on across the world. These disrupting technologies are making some roles redundant and saving time and money with increased accuracy. The challenges brought by these technologies include information security and physical security.

Integration of hardware and software and following standards are the major challenges for the organizations. HR has to find highly skilled integration engineers, which is a tough job. This is also changing the business models of the organizations. Now hardware companies have to charge for software services and software companies have to be paid for hardware, if they involve in pervasive computing. Not everybody can be successful in this area because the organization has to have both hardware and software expertise.

Bibliography/References

Bibliography/References

Alfonso, Bucero (2007), "From Technical Expert to Project Manager", *PM World Today*, Vol. IX, Issue VIII, August.

Alie, S.S. (2015), "Project Governance: #1 Critical Success Factor", Proceeds of the PMI Global Congress, October 11-13, Orlando, Florida, USA.

Al-Sedairy, S.T. (1994), "Management of Conflict: Public Sector Construction in Saudi Arabia", *International Journal of Project Management,* 12(3):143-151.

Anderson Jr., L.L. and Polkinghorn, B. (2008), "Managing Conflict in Construction Mega projects: Leadership and Third-Party Principles", *Conflict Resolution Quarterly,* 26(2): 167-198.

Appelbaum, S.H., Abdallah, C. and Shapiro, B.T. (1999), "The Self-directed Team: A Conflict Resolution Analysis", *Team Performance Management*, 5(2): 60-77.

Armstrong, M. (1984), "A Handbook of Personnel Management Practice", Second Edition, Kogan Page, London.

Art, Koff (2006), "Strategies for Using, Recruiting, Retaining Older Workers", July 20, available at:
www.careermag.com.

Asia Pacific Management News (1999), "What are the Skills of Tomorrow's Global Manager?", Asia Pacific Management Forum, August 4, available at:
www.apmforum.com.

Aswathappa, K. (2005), "Human Resource and Personnel Management", Fourth Edition, Tata McGraw-Hill, New Delhi.

Aswathappa, K. (1996), "Organizational Behaviour", Third Revised and Enlarged Edition, Himalaya Publishing House, New Delhi.

Athreye, S.S. (2005), "The Indian Software Industry and its Evolving Service Capability", *Industrial and Corporate Change,* Vol. 14(3).

Aula, P. and Siira, K. (2010), "Organizational Communication and Conflict Management Systems: A Social Complexity Approach", *Nordicom Review*, 31(1): 125-141.

Avison, D. and Torkzadeh, G. (2009), "Information Systems Project Management", Sage Publications Inc., New York.

Baccarini, D. (1999), "The Logical Framework Method for Defining

Project Success", *Project Management Journal,* Vol. 30, No. 4, 25-32.

Bailey, J.E. and Pearson, S.W. (1983), "Development of a Tool for Measuring and Analyzing Computer User Satisfaction", *Management Science*, Vol. 29, No. 5, 519-529.

Banner, D.K. (1995), "Conflict Resolution: A Recontextualization", *Leadership and Organization Development Journal*, 16(1): 31-34.

Barki, H. and Hartwick, J. (2001), "Interpersonal Conflict and its Management in Information System Development", *MIS Quarterly*, 25(2):195-228, June.

Bartlett, Christopher and Sumantra Ghoshal (2003), "What is a Global Manager?", *Harvard Business Review*, August.

Beleiu, I., Crisan, E. and Nistor, R. (2015), "Main Factors Influencing Project Success", *Interdisciplinary Management Research*, XI, 59-72.

Benjamin, R. (2006), "Project Success as a Function of Project Management Methodology: An Emergent Systems Approach", MBA Thesis, University of Hull, UK, April.

Benta, D., Podean, I.M. and Mircean, C. (2011), "On Best Practices in Risk Management in Complex Projects", *Informatica Economica,* Vol. 15, No. 2, 142-152.

Boynton, A.C. and Zmud, R.W. (1984), "An Assessment of Critical Success Factors", *Sloan Management Review,* Vol. 25, No. 4, 17-27.

Brahnam, S.D., Margavio, T.M., Hignite, M.A., Barrier, T.B. and Chin, J.M. (2005), "A Gender-based Categorization of Conflict Resolution", *Journal of Management Development*, 24(3): 197-208.

Brain, E. Becker and Huselid, Mark A. (2006), "Strategic Human Resources Management: Where Do We Go From Here?", *Journal of Management,* Vol. 32, No. 6, December.

Bullen, C.V. and Rockart, J.F. (1981), "A Primer on Critical Success Factors", CISR No. 69, Sloan Working Paper No. 1220-81, Sloan School of Management, MIT, June.

Churchwell, Cynthia (2003), "The New Global Business Manager: Q&A with Christopher A Bartlett", HBS Working Knowledge, December 15.

Clayton, M. (2016), "What Does Project Governance Really Mean", *Project Manager,* February 17.

Cleland, D.I. and King, W.R. (1983), "Systems Analysis and Project Management", McGraw Hill, New York.

Cooke-Davies, T. (2002), "The Real Success Factors on Projects", *International Journal of Project Management,* Vol. 20, 185-190.

DeLone, W. D. and McLean, E. R. (1992), "Information Systems Success: The Quest for the Dependent Variable," *Information Systems Research*, Vol. 3, No. 1, 60-95.

Du, R., Ai, S. and Brugha, C.M. (2011), "Integrating Taoist Yin-Yang Thinking with Western Nomology: A Moderating Model of Trust in Conflict Management", *Chinese Management Studies,* 5(1): 55-67.

Ellis, C. (2015), "Why Customer Satisfaction is Your Most Important Project Metric", CIO, March 19.

Englund, R. and Bucero, A. (2012), "The Complete Project Manager: Integrating People, Organizational and Technical Skills", Management Concepts Press, Tysons Corner, VA.

Freedman, S. and Katz, L. (2007), "Critical Success Factors for International Projects", *PM World Today*, Vol. IX, No. X, October.

Garemo, N. and Matzinger (2015), "Mega Projects: The Good, The Bad and The Better", *McKinsey and Company,* July.

Gido, J. and Clements, J.P. (1999), "Successful Project Management", South-Western College Publishing, Ohio.

Gupta, N.S. (1997), "Organization: Theory and Behaviour", Third Edition, Himalaya Publishing House, New Delhi.

Guruswamy, M. (2019), "Statue of Unity: Modi Donned Sardar Legacy, and Congress Has 'No Time' for It", *Counter View,* October 31.

Harrin, E. (2016), "7 Factors of Good Project Governance", *Project Management,* strategyex.co.uk, September 8.

Harwardt, M. (2016), "Criteria for Successful IT Projects from Manager's Perspective", *Open Journal of Information Systems*, 3(1), 29-54.

Haughey, D. (2001), "Eight Key Factors to Ensuring Project Success", available at:
www.projectsmart.co.uk.

Heldman, K. (2003), "PMP: Project Management Professional: Study Guide", BPB Publications, New Delhi.

Heller, Jean E. (1980), "Criteria for Selecting an International Manager", *Personnel*, 57, No. 3, May-June, 48.

Holgeid, K. and Thompson M. (2013), "A Refection on Why Large Public Projects Fail?", *Journal of Political Consulting and Policy Advice*, May.

Holland, C.P. and Light, B. (1999), "Critical Success Factor Models for ERP Implementation", *IEEE Software*, Vol. 16, No. 3, 30-36.

Jiang, J. Klein, G. and Balloun, J. (1996), "Ranking of System Implementation Success Factors", *Project Management Journal*, Vol. 27, No. 4, 49-53.

Katzenbach, J.R. and Smith, D.K. (1993), "The Wisdom of Teams", Harvard Business School Press, Boston, MA.

Khan, Adalat (2007), "Global Management Skills", *American Chronicle*, July 31.

Kothari, C.R. (2004), "Research Methodology: Methods and Techniques", Second Edition, New Age International, New Delhi.

Krishnamacharyulu, M. (2012), "Sri Bhagavad Gita", Gita Press, Gorakpur.

Lippitt, G.L. (1982), "Managing Conflicts in Today's Organizations", *Training and Development Journal*, Vol. 36, No. 7, 66-72.

Lock, D. (1984), "Project Management", St. Martins Press, New York.

Marshall, R.A. (2007), "The Contribution of Earned Value Management to Project Success on Contracted Efforts", *Journal of Contract Management*, Summer, 21-33.

Martin, C.C. (1976), "Project Management", Amaco, New York.

May, E.L. and Zimmer, B.A. (1996), "The Evolutionary Development Model for Software", *Hewlett-Packard Journal,* Vol. 47, No. 4, 39-45.

McCarthy, J. (2007), "The State of Development of the IT Services Global Delivery Model", Forrester Research, Inc., Cambridge.

Mehta, Deepshikha (2004), "Are You a Global Manager?", *The Hindu*, December 15.

Meredith, J.R. and Mantel, S.J. (2007), "Project Management: A Managerial Approach", Wiley India, New Delhi.

Mian, D. (2015), "A Model to Assess the Impact of Innovation Activity on Project Performance in Consulting Engineering Firms", Ph.D. Thesis, Queensland University of Technology.

Morris, P.W.G. and Hough, G.H. (1987), "The Anatomy of Major Projects", John Wiley & Sons, New York.

Murali, Balasubramanyam (2007), "RPO: The Killer App in HR Services", *Express Computer*, June 18.

Murray, J.P. (2001), "Recognizing the Responsibility of Failed

Information Technology Project as a Shared Failure", *Information Systems Management*, Vol. 18, No. 2, 25-29.

Nair, N. (2008), "Towards Understanding the Role of Emotions in Conflict: A Review and Future Directions", *International Journal of Conflict Management*, 19(4): 359-381.

Ochieng, E.G. and Price, A.D. (2009), "Framework for Managing Multicultural Project Teams", *Engineering, Construction and Architectural Management*, 16(6): 527-543.

Parisi, C. and Rossi, P. (2015), "Strategic Performance Measurement for Research and Development: A Case Study", *The International Journal of Business & Management,* 3(12), 322-330.

Prabhakar, G.P. (2008), "What is Project Success: A Literature Review", *International Journal of Business and Management,* Vol. 3, No. 9, 3-10.

Prabhudev, Konana (2006), "Can Indian Software Firms Compete with the Global Giants?", *Computer*, IEEE Computer Society, July.

Prasad, L.M. (1994), "Organizational Behaviour", Second Edition, Sultan Chand & Sons, New Delhi.

Raghunadhacharya, S.B. (1992), "Sri Bhagavad Gita", Tirumala Tirupati Devasthanams (TTD), Tirupati.

Ramesh, V., Glass, R. and Vessey, I. (2003), "Research in Computer Science: An Empirical Study", *The Journal of Systems and Software,* Vol. 70, 165-176.

Randolph, W.A. and Posner, B.Z. (1993), "Effective Project Plannning and Management: Getting The Job Done", Prentice-Hall of India Pvt. Ltd, New Delhi.

Reel, J.S. (1999), "Critical Success Factors in Software Projects", *IEEE Software,* Vol. 16, No. 3, 18-23.

Reel, J.S. (1999), "Critical Success Factors in Software Projects", *IEEE Software*, May/June.

Remus, U. and Wiener, M. (2009), "Critical Success Factors for Managing Offshore Software Development Projects", *Journal of Global Information Technology Management*, Vol. 12, No. 1, 06-28.

Robbins, S.P. (2003), "Organization Theory: Structure, Design and Applications", Third Edition, Prentice-Hall of India, New Delhi.

Rockart, J.F. (1979), "Chief Executives Define their Own Data Needs", *Harvard Business Review*, Vol. 57, No. 2, March/April.

Sangwan, R., Bass, M., Mullick, N., Paulish, D.J. and Kazmeier, J. (2006), "Global Software Development Handbook", Auerbach Publications.

Schein, E.H. (1973), "Organizational Psychology", Second Edition, Prentice-Hall of India, New Delhi.

Shank, M.E., Boynton, A.C. and Zmud, R.W. (1985), "Critical Success Factor Analysis as a Methodology for MIS Planning", *MIS Quarterly,* Vol. 9, No. 2, 121-129.

Sivananda, S.S. (1998), "How to Get Vairagya", A Divine Life Society Publication, UP.

Standish Group (1994), "The CHAOS Report", The Standish Group International, Inc., Boston, MA.

Steve, Hamm (2007), "Who's Hiring in America? Indian Firms!", *Business Week*, June 21.

Sudhakar, G.P., Farooq, A. and Patnaik, S. (2011), "Soft Factors Affecting the Performance of Software Development Teams", *Team Performance Management*, 17(3/4): 187-205.

Sudhakar, G.P. and Manjula, G. (2004), "Protecting the Programmer's Productivity", *Businessgyan*, October.

Suresh, Malladi (2008), "Measuring the Software Engineering Productivity: Accounting for the Qualitative Aspects and Pitfalls", *Projects and Profits*, February.

Sutton, Mantel, S., Meredith, J., Shafer, S. and Gopalan, M.R. (2006), "Project Management: Core Text Book", Wiley India Pvt. Ltd.

Turner, J.R. and Müller, R. (2005), "The Project Manager's Leadership Style as a Success Factor on Projects: A Literature Review", *Project Management Journal*, Vol. 36, No. 1, 49-61.

Vaughan, H. (2008), "Challenge of a Program Management Professional", *PM World Today,* Vol. X, Issue IX, 1-6.

Verma, V.K. (1995), "Organizing Projects for Success", Project Management Institute, Newtown Square, PA.

Verma, V.K. (1998), "Conflict Management", in Pinto, J. (ed.), 'Project Management Handbook', Project Management Institute, USA, 1-12.

Verner, J., Cox, K., Bleistein., S. and Cerpa, N. (2005), "Requirements, Engineering and Software Project Success: An Industrial Survey in Australia and the U.S.", *AJIS*, September, 13(1), 225-238.

Walston, C.E. and Felix, C.P. (1977), "A Method of Programming

Measurement and Estimation", *IBM Systems Journal*, Vol. 16, No. 1, 54-73.

Warfield, D. (2010), "IS/IT Research: A Research Methodologies Review", *Journal of Theoretical and Applied Information Technology,* Vol. 13, Issue 1/2, 28-35.

Warner, M. (2000), "Conflict Management in Community-based Natural Resource Projects: Experiences from Fiji and Papua New Guinea", Working Paper No. 135, Overseas Development Institute, London, 1-40.

White, D. and Fortune, J. (2002), "Current Practice in Project Management: An Empirical Study", *International Journal of Project Management,* Vol. 20, 1-11.

Wixom, B.H. (2001), "An Empirical Investigation of the Factors Affecting Data Warehouse Success", *MIS Quarterly,* Vol. 25, No. 1, 17-41.

Wong, B. and Tein, D. (2004), "Critical Success Factors for ERP Projects", *Australian Project Manager,* Vol. 24, No. 1, 28-31.

Yip, Loewe and Yoshino (1988), "How to Take Your Country into the Global Market", *Columbia Journal of Business Review*, Winter.

Yousefi, S., Hipel, K.W. and Hegazy, T. (2010), "Attitude-Based Strategic Negotiation for Conflict Management in Construction Projects", *Project Management Journal*, 41(4): 99-107.

Index

Index